Memories
of a
Midwestern Farm

Memories
of a
Midwestern Farm

GOOD FOOD AND INSPIRATION
FROM AROUND THE KITCHEN TABLE

Nancy Hutchens

ILLUSTRATED BY RICHARD LANG CHANDLER

POCKET BOOKS
New York   London   Toronto   Sydney   Tokyo   Singapore

Use of the following materials is gratefully acknowledged:

Selected Quote from *Mules and Men* by Zora Neale Hurston. Copyright 1935 by Zora Neale Hurston. Copyright renewed 1963 by John C. Hurston and Joel Hurston. Reprinted by permission of HarperCollins Publishers, Inc.

Selected quote from "Hot Weather," in *One Man's Meat* by E. B. White. Copyright 1939 by E. B. White. Reprinted by permission of HarperCollins Publishers, Inc.

Quote by Etta Macy from "Indiana's Self-Reliant Uplanders" by James Alexander Thom, *National Geographic* magazine, Vol. 149, No. 3, March 1976.

"The Ballad of Davy Crockett," collected, adapted and arranged by John A. Lomax and Alan Lomax. Copyright 1934 (Renewed) Ludlow Music, Inc., New York, New York. Used by permission.

"Ole Aunt Kate" and "Old Jesse," from Dorothy Scarborough, *On the Trail of Negro Folk Songs*. Cambridge, Mass.: Harvard University Press. Copyright 1952 by Harvard University Press; copyright renewed 1953 by Mary McDaniel Parker. Reprinted by permission of the publishers.

"Young Man Wouldn't Hoe Corn," from *A Treasury of American Folklore* by B. A. Botkin (editor). Copyright 1944, 1972 by B. A. Botkin. Reprinted by permission of Crown Publishers, Inc.

"The Law of the Yukon," from *The Spell of the Yukon* by Robert Service. Copyright 1916, used by permission of the Estate of Robert Service.

"Hutchens Succeeds on Hills" by Lewis P. East in *The Indiana Farmers Guide,* Vol. 87, June 27, 1931. Permission granted by Farm Progress Companies.

Photograph of Grandpa Hutchens reprinted by permission of M. Anthony Morgan.

POCKET BOOKS, a division of Simon & Schuster Inc.
1230 Avenue of the Americas, New York, NY 10020

Hutchens, Nancy.
   Memories of a midwestern farm : good food and inspiration from
around the kitchen table / Nancy Hutchens.
      p.   cm.
   ISBN: 0-671-51072-X
   1. Cookery, American—Midwestern style.   2. Farm life—Indiana.
I. Title.
TX715.2.M53H88   1995
641.5977—dc20   95-16912
                                                    CIP

First Pocket Books hardcover printing November 1995

10 9 8 7 6 5 4 3 2 1

POCKET and colophon are registered trademarks of
Simon & Schuster Inc.

Book design by Barbara Cohen Aronica

Printed in the U.S.A.

For Mamaw Tribby and Grandpa Hutchens and all of our grandparents—our most devoted teachers and faithful friends.

When I was just a little girl
  you used to care for me.
Were there ever happier times than those,
  just sitting on your knee?
How fast those hours flew,
  we had so much to say.
I'd ask a million questions
  while you told me about your day.
When I grew up and left,
  you knew it was time to part.
But, do you know that I still feel
  you present in my heart?

The author at the age of four.

Nancy Hutchens grew up on a 700-acre farm in the upland hills of southern Indiana, an area of great natural beauty that was settled by frontiersmen who came up through the Cumberland Gap in the first part of the nineteenth century. On her grandfather Hutchens' side of the family she is a descendant of Davy Crockett; her mother's family, the Tribbys, have been in America for eight generations—some in the family say back to the days of the Mayflower. The Tribbys, who settled in Virginia, lived there until 1716 when they went on to Ohio, and then moved farther west to farm in Greene County, Indiana, in 1860.

Nancy's childhood on the farm in the 1950s was reminiscent of life at the turn of the century. Teams of horses were still used for farmwork. Her family used an outhouse until she was eight years old, and it took several more years for television and the telephone to arrive. Soap and butter were made on the farm, and everyday items like blankets and rugs were handmade.

After completing her degrees at Indiana University and Rice University in Houston (where she earned a Ph.D. in anthropology and psychology), Nancy settled in New York City. Since 1985 she has had her own business, consulting to companies about human resources. Nancy and her husband, Michael Fields, live in Westchester County, New York, but she still considers Indiana home.

ACKNOWLEDGMENTS

Like a lot of people, I'd pick up a book in the bookstore and think, I could do this. Until I was knee-deep in writing this book, I had no idea how many people, working together as a team, it takes to make a book. This book would be incomplete without mention of those I was lucky enough to have working with me.

Janis Vallely, who is much more of a friend than an agent, navigated me through the mysterious world of book publishing. Janis helped to mold this book and guided me in rediscovering the voice of the farm girl buried underneath the citified adult.

Richard Lang Chandler communicated my feelings and memories visually through his drawings, which depict all family farms and bring us back to this vanishing way of life. Richard's endless stream of creative ideas is seen throughout these pages.

Claire Zion, my editor, completely shared my vision of this book and gave me the freedom to explore ideas. Working with her was a joy.

Daddy—Joseph Wilbur Hutchens—supported me in all stages of writing this memoir about our family life, even though he is one of the few people in America not interested in publicity. He checked the accuracy of my childhood recollections as they pertained to farming.

My nephews, Michael Hutchens and Philip Morgan, poured over microfilm in search of lost articles. My aunts, Esther (Tribby) Borden and Pauline Hutchens Burch; my cousins, Leon Weaver and Carla Tidd; and Daddy, Sue, and Jeff tracked down memorabilia for me.

Sue, Alan, and Jeff and their families continue to do the most important work—keeping these memories alive and passing them on to the next generation.

Michael Fields, my husband, understood how much writing this book meant to me. He accepted, without blinking an eye, weeks of strange meals consisting of nothing but desserts or apple dishes or stews, and many lonely evenings.

The recipes I've included here were the ones we used on our farm but they belong to the people of the upland hills of southern

Indiana. It has always seemed to me that this region is blessed with an inordinately large number of exceptional cooks who have been preparing these dishes their entire lives. I want to thank these wonderful women who enrich the lives of everyone who knows them. One of these women was my mother, Veva (Tribby) Hutchens.

Mother's presence was with me throughout writing this book. Through teaching me how to cook she taught me about life.

CONTENTS

INTRODUCTION

The Simple Pleasures of Life on the Farm

'Tis the gift to be simple,
'Tis the gift to be free,
'Tis the gift to come down
Where we ought to be.
And when we find ourselves
in the place just right,
'Twill be in the valley of
love and delight.

—Simple Gifts, Shaker song, 1848

THROUGH THE FARMHOUSE DOOR

Let's sit in the old-fashioned parlor again
And let me take hold of your hand.
The light will be low—and I'll whisper the words
That bring dreams of days spent on the land.
A branch, a farmhouse with winding rock paths—
Let's pause for a glance through its door.
A family around an old wooden table,
And Mother fills our plates with s'more.

—Mamaw Tribby (1936)

I grew up in the fifties in Little Cincinnati, Indiana. Little Cincinnati was a village in the Indiana upland hills with a fire tower, ten houses, two churches, a one-room schoolhouse, and our family farm. Everyone thought we were rich because we had land. I thought we were poor because my dad never got a regular paycheck. The fire tower was the closest I ever came to seeing a skyscraper until I was about twelve. It was built on land that my grandpa, Harlan Crockett Hutchens, had leased to the state for a dollar for one hundred years. Grandpa Hutchens was a smart and cantankerous farmer who never went inside a church building except to go to funerals. Working in the fields every day, surrounded by the power and beauty of Mother Nature, was enough for him.

As a little girl, I could look down from the fire tower to see field after field of land—wheat, corn, or soybeans in the summer, dried stalks waiting to be chopped up into silage for cattle feed in the fall, and the silent bare earth in the winter. At the base of the tower were Daddy and Grandpa's enormous vegetable gardens—each over a quarter of an acre. The rows of tasseled corn at the very back were followed by stakes of tomato plants and "pole" beans, and then, the vines— the low-growing strawberries, cucumbers, and potatoes—in the front.

Gardening was serious business. Almost all of the food we ate throughout the year came from the land. We had few luxuries—television, telephones, and indoor bathrooms didn't reach us until I was almost a teenager—but our kitchen table was filled with luscious, natural food. Working in the fields was the strict preserve of the men in our family, while the women did the cooking, but we came together to work in the garden and to break bread around the kitchen table. Each of us, from my baby brother Jeffrey to Daddy, helped to grow the food we ate throughout the year. All of us staked the tomatoes when they grew heavy on the vine, hoed the bunch beans, and shared the everyday weeding and watering of the garden. We all were proud when the kitchen table was loaded down with our own homegrown fruits, vegetables, and herbs.

When I was ten, Grandpa built a new home and Mother was busy for weeks sprucing up his wonderful old farmhouse, which our family had inherited. To help her out, I began cooking. My very first meal—Harvard beets, creamed peas, fried potatoes, and pork chops—was colorful but not very inspired. By the time I was fourteen, I was cooking meals for hay hands and making Sunday dinners that were second to none in the county.

My mother was both a vegetable gardener and a great cook. She taught me to honor food and that the ability to prepare it was a divine gift we all have. Mother always knew that cooking is a celebration of life. This little book is a collection of memories about gardening and cooking with my family in the upland hills of southern Indiana. It is a way to share with you the simple recipes and pleasures that have been a part of our life on the farm for many generations.

Mother's Five Golden Rules of Cooking

1 Cook with Love

Love is the secret ingredient that gives food its essence—the flavor that stays with you long after the dishes are washed. The simple memory of Mother's apron hanging on a nail on the back porch, waiting for her to start supper, still floods me with warm feelings. She believed that the fanciest dish prepared in anger was not satisfying, while food prepared with love—even a washday meal of cabbage and corn fritters—was sublime.

2 Make Your Kitchen a Sanctuary for Everyone

Mother used to say that the kitchen is the heart of the home. Daddy, Grandpa, my brothers, neighbors, and playmates were always passing through the kitchen, tempted by the smell of coffee perking and something good in the oven. No one was ever told to leave the kitchen because we were "busy" cooking. Many times when I asked Mother how good my bread or pot roast was, she would smile and say, "You'll know you're a great cook when people can't stay out of your kitchen."

3 Start with the Best Fruits and Vegetables

When you grow your own food, you know exactly how it was treated. Like children, food thrives on love. We can't have fresh garden produce all year round, but we can enjoy home-canned products with their own unique flavors and textures.

◆ ◆

4 USE RECIPES AS SUGGESTIONS, NOT FORMULAS

Mother wasn't concerned about following recipes; instead, she taught me how to communicate with food—to listen to it, and feel it. "The bread will tell you when you've kneaded enough," she would say. "You have to look at the corn today because it's more mature than what we had last week. A recipe won't tell you the difference."

5 USE YOUR HANDS WHEN YOU CAN

Our electric mixer didn't do much good when we cooked for hay hands or had family get-togethers. Mother would stick her hand up to the elbow in a big bowl of coleslaw or potato salad and stir. You may not need to cook in such large quantities, but remember, like any living thing, food would rather be stroked by a human hand than beaten with a metal whip. Or as Mother put it, "Don't be afraid to touch it if your hands are clean. Just think how much happier anybody is when they get a pat."

◆ ◆

A Word About Farm Cooking

I'm told, in riding somewhere West,
A stranger found a Hoosier's nest . . .
One side was lined with divers garments,
The other spread with skins of "varmints";
Dried pumpkins overhead were strung,
Where venison hams in plenty hung;
Two rifles placed above the door;
Three dogs lay stretched upon the floor—
In short, the domicile was rife
With specimens of Hoosier life.

> —John Finley,
> "The Hoosier's Nest" (1830)

*F*arm cookery as we know it in southern Indiana comes from the pioneers who settled the area in the early to middle 1800s. Some, like my great-grandmother Belle Crockett's family, came up from the South. She descended from Davy's brother after he left Tennessee and moved to Indiana. They were great hunters and backwoodsmen. Other settlers, like Mother's family, the Tribbys, were farmers from the East. My grandmother, Mamaw Tribby, used to tell us handed-down stories about how they started homesteading in Indiana in 1860 after leaving Germany in the early 1600s and living for several generations in Virginia and Ohio.

Our pioneer ancestors lived in log cabins with a big open fireplace for cooking. A Dutch oven, like the ones we still use, simmered over the fire with a squirrel or rabbit stew in it. If fruit was in season, they might be lucky enough to have a big slice of apple or raspberry pie. For special occasions they made wonderful dishes from native plants, such as the persimmon, huckleberry, hickory nut, and sassafras. I've included the original recipes here so you can try them for yourself.

On a typical day on the farm our men herded cattle, mended fences, and plowed, while we made bread, churned butter, and washed clothes. Meat, cream, butter, and sugar gave us the energy to do this work day in and day out. Few of us today have the same physical need for hearty cooking, but more than ever we crave the emotional sustenance of old-fashioned country food. Nothing makes the morning a little perkier, the day a little brighter, or the night a little warmer than sitting around the kitchen table with a home-cooked meal filled with good stuff from the garden and oven.

Most farm families had at least one milk cow for their own use and one milker. Not everyone has the right touch to milk a cow, but Grandpa Hutchens was the best milker in our family. Every morning, whether it was a Sunday or the Fourth of July, he set a pail of milk on the back porch in time for breakfast. The raw milk was hand separated, and it produced three types of dairy for cooking and drinking. The top layer was the heavy cream, so thick you could eat it with a spoon. This was what we made butter out of. The next layer was more like store-bought cream diluted with a little half-and-half—we called this "top milk." Under that was the regular milk that we drank. Overall, it was rich, a little richer than store-bought whole milk. The exact flavor of fresh, raw milk can't be replicated, but you can approximate it by mixing a little half-and-half into whole milk.

Nothing in the world compares with butter—made in a wooden churn from the milk of your favorite Guernsey—slathered on a piece of fresh yeasty bread still warm from the oven. But I hate to tell you: that butter has very little in common with the butter we reach for in a supermarket. Like most people who farmed in the Indiana hills, we often used margarine unless we had homemade butter. Store-bought butter was expensive and did not taste like "real" butter to us.

As far as I am concerned, all of the dishes described here can be made either with butter or with margarine, and any kind of milk will do. If you are concerned about cholesterol, here are some easy variations you might try. Substitute skim milk for whole milk or cream. And in most dishes other than baked goods, you can reduce the amount of fat by about a quarter and use unsaturated vegetable oil. In all cases, use your judgment: the most important thing is to make these recipes fit your diet. Then you can enjoy them every day—instead of saving them just for special occasions.

THE TRIBBY FAMILY ALBUM

The Tribbys shortly after they came to Indiana; probably taken in the 1870s.

Early pioneer ancestors on Mamaw Tribby's side of the family.

Four generations of Tribby women at the turn of the century. Mamaw Tribby is on the right, holding Mary, her next-to-oldest daughter.

SPRING

The Glory
of the
Early Garden

Behold, my brothers, the spring has come;
the earth has received the embraces of the sun and
we shall soon see the results of that love!
Every seed is awakened and so has all animal life.

—Sitting Bull

A Spring Meal to Feed the Hungry Farmer

*We went out to the garden and found everything
thriving. . . . We picked heads of the most beautiful
lettuce you ever saw, and we cut asparagus.
Then we came in and washed the asparagus,
steamed it, and had a feast of asparagus and
lettuce not half an hour out of the garden.*

—Hal Borland,
Hal Borland's Book of Days

As soon as the fields began to dry after the spring rains and the first plants popped up through the earth the whole farm became a shimmering green. We savored the special dishes made of delicate spring vegetables—like leaf lettuce, asparagus, and new peas—that have long been a part of the farmer's tradition. Buttery-soft leaf lettuce came from the front rows of the garden by the basketfuls. Each leaf had to be looked over carefully to make sure no bugs would make their way into a salad. Big mounds of lettuce mixed with scallions were "wilted" with a hot dressing in a cast-iron skillet. Wilted lettuce had been a family favorite for generations, probably some version of a dish brought by the original Tribby settlers from Germany in the seventeenth century.

The potato plants were ready to flower, which meant that the earth underneath was bursting with baby reds, and our new sweet peas were bulging in their jackets. Daddy's special pride was growing the most delicate, sweetest Irish potatoes in the county. We cooked them in the skins with new peas in light cream sauce. Unlike vegetables from the garden that grew in full summer—corn, tomatoes, cucumbers, and green beans—wilted lettuce and new peas and potatoes were more difficult to cook the way the family liked them. Many springs passed before I could turn out an early-garden dinner exactly like Mother's.

The farm bustled and hummed with activity. During dinner, the noon meal, the talk around the kitchen table was serious: what equipment needed to be repaired, how much longer would it take to finish a field, how did the ground feel, did someone need to go to the feed store for more seed. Mother and I knew that the meal we served was the best part of the day. It was our way of showing how much we appreciated the spring labors of the men in the family.

There's no sight on earth more appealing than the sight of a woman making dinner for someone she loves.

—Thomas Wolfe

Daddy being helped by Aunt Pauline and Sue on a spring day in 1941.

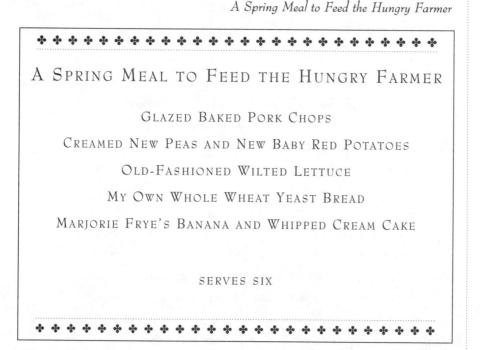

A SPRING MEAL TO FEED THE HUNGRY FARMER

GLAZED BAKED PORK CHOPS

CREAMED NEW PEAS AND NEW BABY RED POTATOES

OLD-FASHIONED WILTED LETTUCE

MY OWN WHOLE WHEAT YEAST BREAD

MARJORIE FRYE'S BANANA AND WHIPPED CREAM CAKE

SERVES SIX

GLAZED BAKED PORK CHOPS

✦   Wash and dry 6 thick-cut (1½-inch) pork chops. Rub each side of each pork chop with a little more than a pinch of ground ginger and a tablespoon of brown sugar. Salt and arrange side by side in a baking dish. Cover the pan and bake for 30 minutes at 350°.

Add 2 tablespoons of Worcestershire sauce into a ½ cup of boiling water and pour over the chops. Bake for another 10 minutes, uncovered.

Turn over and cook for another 5 minutes or until tender. Pour the pan drippings into a skillet and simmer, adding 1 tablespoon of cornstarch. Stir and, when thickened, serve over the pork chops.

CREAMED NEW PEAS AND NEW BABY RED POTATOES

✦   How often Mother and I would come up from the garden, our gathering baskets brimming over with fresh-picked peas! We rocked back and forth in the big wooden swing on the back porch as we shelled them. Toward the end of their season, when we were short on peas, we stretched this dish by adding more new baby red potatoes.

Shell enough new peas to make 3 cups. Thoroughly wash about 14 small new red potatoes but don't peel them. (Usually the smaller they are, the more delicate the flavor.) In a saucepan, boil the potatoes and peas in water until barely tender, about 20 minutes, depending on the size of the potatoes. Drain in a colander and set aside.

In a large saucepan, make a cream sauce by melting 4 table-spoons of butter and gradually adding 4 tablespoons of flour, stirring it in, one spoon at a time. Cook over a low heat, stirring until the lumps disappear. Add 3 cups of milk, one cup at a time, and mix with the flour. Let it simmer and thicken, stirring constantly, for about 5 minutes. Add the peas and potatoes and simmer, stirring frequently, until the peas are tender and the sauce reaches the desired thickness. (The exact cooking time for the peas will vary, depending on their size and toughness. Check them frequently.) Our family always liked this dish made fairly thick, with the cream sauce about the consistency of a milk shake. Season with salt and pepper.

OLD-FASHIONED WILTED LETTUCE

✦   This is best made with fresh-picked leaf lettuce, carefully looked over, washed, dried, and cut into 1-inch strips. If garden lettuce isn't available, you can use store-bought red or green leaf lettuce.

In a 1½-gallon crock or ceramic bowl, mound the lettuce, making sure it doesn't reach all the way to the top of the bowl. Chop up

4 or 5 scallions, including the crisp part of the green tops, and scatter them on top of the lettuce. Sprinkle salt and pepper on top.

Find a cast-iron skillet that will seal tightly if you invert it over the bowl containing the lettuce. Make sure the bowl will support the weight of the skillet and won't shatter from heat. If a cast-iron skillet is too heavy for you to work with, use a lighter-weight skillet. However, it is essential that you cover the lettuce with the skillet you cook with to get the lettuce hot enough to wilt.

Slowly fry 5 or 6 slices of bacon in the skillet until very crisp. Remove the bacon and crumble it over the lettuce.

Combine 1 cup of cider vinegar with 1/2 cup of water. Add gradually and carefully to the hot bacon grease. Add 1/3 cup of sugar and stir until the mixture comes to a rolling boil. Make sure it is very hot all the way through and the sugar has dissolved. Pour the dressing over the lettuce and quickly toss. Immediately invert the skillet over the bowl. Let it set for at least 5 or 6 minutes to give the lettuce time to wilt. Toss again before serving.

MY OWN WHOLE WHEAT YEAST BREAD

✦ Since I was a little girl, I have always made bread in one of the beautiful, deep-blue crocks that have been made in the little town of Clay City, Indiana, for over a hundred years. My favorite one was one of Mother's wedding presents, and I was always very careful not to chip it. To this day, I'm afraid my bread won't taste the same if I don't use the blue bowl.

Heat 2 cups of milk to scalding (a skin will form, but don't let it boil), add 3 tablespoons of butter, 2 teaspoons of salt, and 1/3 cup of unfiltered honey. Cool to lukewarm in a big ceramic bowl.

Dissolve 2 tablespoons of dry yeast in 1/2 cup lukewarm water. After it sets for 5 minutes or so, add it to the lukewarm milk mixture in the bowl. Add 3/4 cup of wheat germ, 1 teaspoon of salt, and start stirring in flour with a wooden spoon. (I would suggest using about 4

cups of whole wheat flour and 2 cups of unbleached white flour. Bread made with only whole wheat flour is very dense and not as "yeasty." The more white flour you use the more the bread will rise.) Keep adding white flour and stirring as long as you can until the dough is too stiff to stir. Altogether you will need about 6 cups of flour. When the dough starts to pull away from the sides, start kneading it in the bowl with your hands. Continue adding flour until it is no longer sticky. Turn it out onto a floured board and continue kneading until the bread is very elastic and smooth. This will take about 10 minutes, or 300 turns. Don't compromise on the kneading—it's the secret to great homemade bread. If you have any doubt, keep going.

Put the dough in a greased bowl and turn it over so the greased side is up. Cover it with a clean, damp cloth and let it rise for about an hour, or until it doubles in size. Punch it down, knead it a few times, cover it and let it double again.

Separate the dough into two loaves, place them in greased loaf pans and cover them. Let rise until the dough doubles—about 45 minutes.

If you like, you can glaze the top with an egg wash (1 beaten egg mixed with a little cold water). Bake in a preheated 375° oven for 45 minutes or until the bread is browned. If you tap it and hear a hollow sound, it's done.

> *Ole Aunt Kate she bake a cake,*
> *She bake it behind the garden gate,*
> *She sift de meal, she gimme de dust,*
> *She bake de bread, she gimme de crust . . .*
>
> —folk song

MARJORIE FRYE'S BANANA AND WHIPPED CREAM CAKE

✦   Marjorie Frye was a wonderful friend to Mother and still is one of the best cooks you'll find anywhere. Although she became renowned for her pies when she made them for J&J's, a little diner at the junction of State Roads 45 and 445, we were always partial to her cakes. This cake was the one we usually picked for birthdays.

Cream together 2 cups of sugar and 1 cup of soft butter. Sift together 4 level cups of cake flour and 4 teaspoons of baking powder. Beat 4 egg whites until foamy. Mash 2 large ripe bananas. Add the dry ingredients to the butter-and-sugar mixture, alternating with 1⅓ cups of milk and the beaten egg whites. Mix in the mashed bananas. Beat well. Fold in 1 cup of walnut pieces.

Grease and flour three 9-inch cake pans. Bake in a moderate oven (350°) until browned on top, 30 to 40 minutes. Insert a broom straw or toothpick in the middle to check for doneness.

To make the filling, gently heat ½ cup of cream in a double boiler until warm, but not boiling. In a small bowl, mix together 1½ tablespoons of flour with 3 tablespoons of sugar; add 3 egg yolks and ¼ cup of cream and stir until smooth. Slowly add the egg mixture to the heated cream and cook until it thickens enough to not drip down the sides of the cake—about the consistency of cake batter. When it cools completely, in an hour or so, stir in 2 mashed large ripe bananas.

Spread the filling in between the layers. Ice the cake with sweetened whipped cream or Chocolate Icing (see page 87). Decorate with fresh whole strawberries around the base of the cake and on the top. This cake will keep better with the chocolate icing. Whipped cream is delicious but needs to stay cold and shouldn't be eaten after two days.

How Grandpa Started the Farm

Soil was a living body. Tom respected it as such. . . .
Tom doubted if anyone who wasn't born on a farm could
understand how he felt about the land.
"Why, hell," they'd say, "it's just a piece of dirt."
It was more than that to him. . . . But he couldn't explain it. . . .
He was a happy man.

—Richard Rhodes, *Farm*

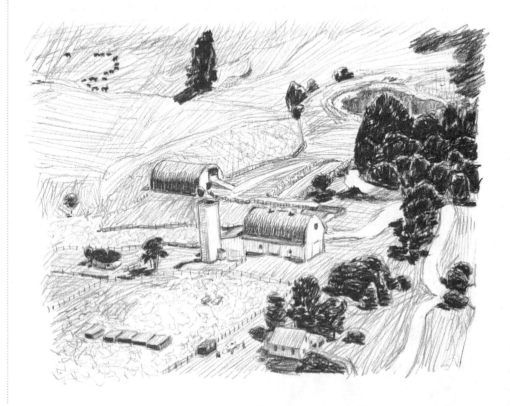

Grandpa believed that the farming way of life was the soul of America. In June of 1931, in the middle of the Depression, *The Indiana Farmer's Guide,* a monthly farming magazine, wrote the following article about Grandpa Hutchens and our farm. It was titled "Hutchens Succeeds on Hills." The beautiful, rocky hills of southern Indiana may nurture the soul, but they are hard on the plow. Grandpa Hutchens, who loved a challenge, always said that if you thought first, planned what you wanted to do, and stuck with it, you could do just about anything. By the time he died, in 1973, the farm had grown to about 700 acres with three big, comfortable houses and several large barns on it. But, most important, it was home to eleven people and more cows, pigs, dogs, cats, rabbits, squirrels, and raccoons than you could count.

> *Write it down that here I labored,*
> *Here I sang and laughed and neighbored.*
> *Write it down when I have perished*
> *That my every thought and act*
> *Was to keep this farm intact.*
>
> —Mamaw Tribby

The Indiana
Farmers Guide

87th Year
Established in 1845

| Volume 87 | Huntington, Indiana, June 27, 1931 | Number 26 |

HUTCHENS SUCCEEDS ON HILLS

Harlan Crockett Hutchens, farmer, living in the eastern part of Greene County, Indiana, is proving to himself and others that it is still possible to make a little money—at least enough to enable himself and family to enjoy life—on a southern Indiana hill farm. Having once tried farming, his young man's quest for adventure drew him to the wheat fields of the West where he worked for awhile. Later he obtained employment in a railroad shop in Kansas. But, finally he felt the desire for some good old Greene county dirt under his feet again and so he came back and purchased his present 240-acre farm in 1920.

It was a pretty poor specimen at that time. The house was gradually tumbling down and there was a "ramshackle" barn. The soil was considered poor and there were no good fences. Probably the most valuable asset was a few acres of standing timber, part of which was usable.

However, during the past eleven years since he bought the place, with the aid of some standing timber and some old timbers taken from the tumbling down house and barn, he has built a new house with a furnace and other modern conveniences, a new bank barn and a poultry house with a capacity for 800 hens. Being a good carpenter, he did most of the work himself, only hiring a helper part of the time. A hired hand took care of the farm while this building was taking place. Other improvements include liming of 27 acres—part of it twice—and by use of manure and legumes the soil has been put in a fair state of fertility. . . .

An idea of this successful hill farmer's present cropping system can be grasped by the fact that this year he has sown 35 acres of mixed timothy and clover, 2 acres of alfalfa, 26 acres of corn and 27 acres of oats. His rotation is corn, oats, clover and timothy two years, and alfalfa on the side.

In regard to the productiveness of this hill farm, Mr. Hutchens states that after having applied poultry manure over most of it and after having grown legumes for several years, he can expect an average of at least fifty bushels of corn per acre. One year he raised one-third of an acre of Irish potatoes. From this he got enough for his family's use and sold $135 worth in addition. He then increased his acreage of potatoes for several years until at one time he was producing 4 acres. One year his potatoes made him enough to buy a truck.

Possibly one of the reasons Mr. Hutchens has been so successful is the fact that he has not tried to do more than he and his 15-year old son can do and do well. That is one of his secrets, it would seem. Everything he does has first been planned out. This is exemplified by the way he manages his time. . . . He spends most of his time right there on the farm and has found that this is the only way he can expect to keep ahead of his work. He says that once he was farming 45 acres and thought he had all he could take care of. Since then, however, he has learned that by properly managing his time he can handle many more acres with little more work than he exerted on the 45-acre farm.

Grandpa waving goodbye at the end of a long day in the fields in June 1970.

Jeff's Special Backwoodsman's Breakfast

Enter these enchanted woods,
You who dare.

—George Meredith,
 "The Woods of the Westermain"

*T*he woods behind the house were filled with beautiful and mysterious plants, like ginseng and sassafras, but nothing could compare with the wild mushrooms we found in April. Webbed on the outside, with a savory, nutty flavor on the inside, they were triangular shapes that could grow to almost a foot in height. We just called them mushrooms—although their real name is morels. While it was still damp from the spring thaw, they would sprout under a tree trunk hidden from sight, where ordinary people like me couldn't find them. A person who had the gift—in our family that was my brother Jeff—would go out with a bucket and come back in no time with hundreds of mushrooms and tall tales about finding so many he couldn't carry them all. Other people made serious enemies by boasting about all the mushrooms they'd had for breakfast to someone who didn't have anyone in their family with the gift. Jeff's gift didn't come out until I was seventeen and he was about ten. Until then we were lucky to have enough mushrooms for one decent meal each spring.

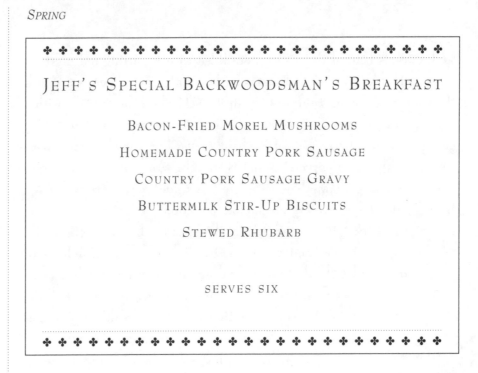

JEFF'S SPECIAL BACKWOODSMAN'S BREAKFAST

BACON-FRIED MOREL MUSHROOMS

HOMEMADE COUNTRY PORK SAUSAGE

COUNTRY PORK SAUSAGE GRAVY

BUTTERMILK STIR-UP BISCUITS

STEWED RHUBARB

SERVES SIX

BACON-FRIED MOREL MUSHROOMS

✦ Wild mushrooms were cooked in only one way—dredged in cornmeal and then fried to a golden brown in bacon fat. Ideally, you should plan on 3 to 5 mushrooms, depending on their size, per person.

Split the mushrooms in half. First, soak them for at least a couple of hours in salted water to draw out any bugs that might be hiding in the webbing. Pat them dry. Slightly beat 3 eggs with a tablespoon of milk. Dip each mushroom in the egg batter and then dredge in cornmeal. Fry in a cast-iron skillet of hot bacon fat until golden brown on all sides. Drain and serve them crisp and crunchy.

HOMEMADE COUNTRY PORK SAUSAGE

✦ Like most country people, when we butchered a pig, we used a metal grinder that had been in the family forever to make our own sausage and mincemeat (see page 157). The grinder clamped on to the side of the kitchen table so that the handle could turn. A metal pan under it caught the ground meat. My brother Alan turned it while Mother pushed the meat through to the blades with a small wooden spoon.

Use 1 pound of side pork to make about 4 medium-size sausage patties. We usually made about 5 pounds—enough for about 20 patties. Cut the pork into small pieces and grind it coarsely. Season it with 2 teaspoons of sage, 2 teaspoons of salt, 2 teaspoons of coarse-ground pepper, and ¹/₂ teaspoon of ground allspice. If you want it hot, you can add ¹/₂ teaspoon of crushed red pepper flakes (or to taste). Mix it with your hands, and then put it through the grinder again using the fine disk.

Fry the patties slowly, with no added fat, in a 10-inch cast-iron skillet until they are nice and brown. Drain them on paper towels. Fry 1 patty per person plus a couple of extra and freeze the rest.

COUNTRY PORK SAUSAGE GRAVY

✦ Use the same skillet you fried the sausage patties in. The sausage drippings should completely cover the bottom of the skillet. Make sure the drippings are very hot and stir in 3 tablespoons of flour. Cook the flour in the drippings to brown it and stir out the lumps. Turn the heat to low and gradually add 3 cups of milk, stirring constantly. Cook until it boils and thickens to the consistency you like. Salt and pepper.

Another way of making it is to fry the sausage in chunks instead of patties and make the gravy with the meat in it or keep one of the extra patties "for the pan." Just break it up with a spatula to make a meatier gravy. This will yield 3¹/₂ cups of gravy. I like to have at least a ¹/₂ cup per person.

> *I love my wife, I love my baby,*
> *I love my biscuits sopped in gravy.*
> *All I want to make me happy,*
> *Two little boys to call me pappy.*

— "Black-Eyed Susie," a fiddle song

BUTTERMILK STIR-UP BISCUITS

✦   Measure 2 heaping cups of flour. Sift together with ½ teaspoon of baking soda, 2½ teaspoons of baking powder, and ½ teaspoon of salt. Lightly cut in 3 tablespoons of butter, until the mixture has a pebbly consistency. Add about 1 cup of buttermilk or as much as you need to make a soft dough. (If you don't have buttermilk on hand, add a teaspoon of vinegar to the milk and let it set for a minute.) If the dough is too wet to handle, sprinkle a little flour on it. Handle it as little as possible—it will still be lumpy.

Turn out the dough onto a floured board and roll or pat it out to about ½ inch thick. Cut with a biscuit cutter or glass (2½ inches in diameter) dipped in flour. Bake with the sides barely touching on an ungreased baking sheet in a hot (425°) oven for 10 to 15 minutes, or until brown. Yields about a dozen biscuits.

STEWED RHUBARB

✦   Rhubarb seemed to grow wild in the hills on the farm, but it had been started by Mamaw Tribby right after Mother and Daddy were married. While it was still tender, Mother cooked it almost every day and kept it on the kitchen table in a dark-blue glass bowl. Delicious at room temperature or cold, stewed rhubarb is also wonderful on bread, with milk, or as a separate dish.

Using the tenderest pink stalks, cut up enough rhubarb into 1-inch pieces to measure 2 cups. Put into a saucepan and add $1/3$ cup of water (to keep it from scorching until its juices come out). Stir in sugar to taste (about $1^1/_2$ cups). Since rhubarb takes quite a bit of sugar, add the juice of 1 lemon and a dash of salt to keep it from tasting syrupy. A pinch of sweet spice, such as cinnamon, nutmeg, or mace, adds a nice flavor. Cook over a low heat until the sugar dissolves, and then bring it quickly to a boil. Add 2 tablespoons of cornstarch and stir. Continue to boil until the juices become translucent, usually 3 to 5 minutes. (The time it takes depends on the tenderness of the rhubarb.) Stop cooking immediately by setting the pan in a sinkful of cold water so you don't loose the wonderful pink color. When cool, it should be the consistency of thin preserves. Serve it warm or cold. It keeps on the table for a day and for several days in the refrigerator. This will yield about 3 cups.

When you gather rhubarb, pull young stalks from the ground and use them immediately. The sugar and flavor are rapidly lost after pulling. *Carefully dispose of the leaves, which are poisonous.* Every time I went out to pull some rhubarb, Mother warned me not to drop the leaves where our dog, Myffles (who wasn't very bright) might find them.

> *When a man's stomach is full it makes no difference whether he is rich or poor.*
>
> —Euripides

Strawberries Three Meals a Day

In the dooryard fronting an old farm-house near the
    white-wash'd palings,
Stands the lilac-bush tall-growing with heart-shaped leaves
    of rich green,
With many a pointed blossom rising delicate, with the
    perfume strong I love . . .

      —Walt Whitman,
          "When Lilacs Last in the Dooryard Bloom'd"

Home—the farmhouse built by Grandpa Hutchens, as it looked in 1953.

'Long about knee-deep in June,
'Bout the time strawberries melts
On the vine.

—James Whitcomb Riley,
"Knee-Deep in June"

*I*n the spring of 1925, right after the farmhouse was finished, my Grandmother Flo planted purple lilac bushes on either side of the back door and then set out her first patch of strawberries. Thirty-five years later, we moved into the big white house with its three big porches and stone steps. By then the lilac bushes had almost eclipsed the entrance to the porch that led to the barnyard. Every May their heavy fragrance floated into the living room and kitchen through the open doors and windows to remind us that spring was in her prime. The first glorious morning that the lilacs opened enough to cut, I raced into the house to get Mother, who loved them above all other flowers. She'd stop frying pancakes or scrambling eggs long enough to make up a bouquet for me to take to school and another one for the breakfast table. At the same time, the sweet old-fashioned strawberries were turning bright red and we couldn't stop eating them: plain, sugared with shortcake, in homemade ice cream, or—the biggest and most perfect ones—in pies. Every time I'd walk by the garden, I'd stop and eat them straight from the vine. Almost every day when we were "in" the strawberries, Mother would make a biscuit shortcake and we'd eat it at breakfast, dinner, and supper. The only thing more wonderful than strawberries and lilacs was knowing that summer was around the corner.

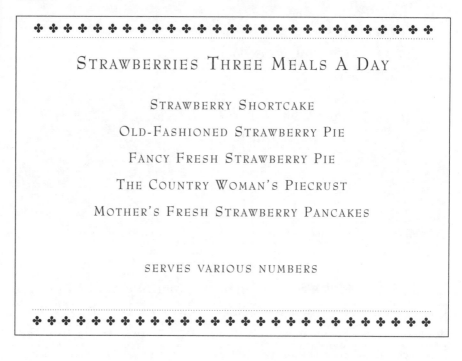

✤ ✤

STRAWBERRIES THREE MEALS A DAY

STRAWBERRY SHORTCAKE

OLD-FASHIONED STRAWBERRY PIE

FANCY FRESH STRAWBERRY PIE

THE COUNTRY WOMAN'S PIECRUST

MOTHER'S FRESH STRAWBERRY PANCAKES

SERVES VARIOUS NUMBERS

✤ ✤

STRAWBERRY SHORTCAKE

✦   Chop about 2 quarts of stemmed and washed strawberries so that each berry is cut into about eighths. Add sugar to taste, about 3/4 cup. Set aside to let the sugar make a syrup. (Although the strawberries aren't quite so pretty cut up this small, they make more syrup and the pieces will snuggle between the layers of shortcake.)

Sift together 3 cups of unbleached flour, 3 tablespoons of sugar, 3 1/2 teaspoons of baking powder, and 1/2 teaspoon of salt. Cut in 1/4 cup of cold butter with a pastry blender and stir in 1 cup of cream or half-and-half. Make a dough and divide it in half.

Pat or roll out each piece of dough so that it will fit into a greased, 9-inch square pan. Flour your hands and sprinkle the dough with enough flour to work it, but try not to handle it more than necessary. Fit the first piece into the pan and brush the top with melted butter. Carefully pick up the other square of dough and put it on top of the bottom piece of dough. Bake in a preheated 450° oven for 20 to 30 minutes, or until lightly browned.

While still warm, cut the shortcake into 3-inch squares. Pull the two layers apart just enough to make a pocket. Spoon the strawberries into the pocket and over the top, making sure to use enough syrup so that the shortcake isn't dry. Serve with sweetened whipped cream or vanilla ice cream. This is best served warm, but also delicious at room temperature. Serves nine.

OLD-FASHIONED STRAWBERRY PIE

✦   Use a quart of strawberries for each pie you want to make. Wash, stem, and cut them into halves. For each quart of strawberries, cover with about ³/₄ cup of sugar, or to taste. Mix with ¹/₃ cup of flour and pour into an unbaked pie shell (see the piecrust recipe, page 34). Dot with 2 tablespoons of butter. Cover with a solid or lattice-weaved crust. Bake in a preheated 425° oven until the pastry is lightly browned, about 45 minutes.

FANCY FRESH STRAWBERRY PIE

✦   Pick a quart of the largest and most perfect strawberries you can find. Stem and wash them but leave them whole. When they are dry, pick out those that are about the same size and arrange them in an attractive pattern, pointed ends up, on a prebaked, single piecrust (see the following recipe). About three quarters of the berries should fill the piecrust.

Coarsely chop the remaining berries—this should make about a cup. Combine the chopped strawberries and a cup of sugar in a saucepan and set over a medium heat. Dissolve 3 tablespoons of cornstarch in $1/2$ cup of cold water and add a dash of lemon juice. Pour the mixture over the berries and sugar and stir constantly until the liquid boils, thickens, and turns transparent. After allowing it to cool a little (about 20 minutes—but keep an eye on it and don't let it get too thick to pour), glaze the whole berries in the piecrust with this liquid. (Don't use the chunks of cooked berries, because then the pie doesn't look as pretty. You can save them to use as a sauce over ice cream.) Drizzle the liquid glaze over the berries, using it to fill in the holes, and use a pastry brush to make sure the glaze covers the berries.

Chill the pie for 2 hours. Top each individual serving with sweetened whipped cream.

THE COUNTRY WOMAN'S PIECRUST

✦   For every double-crusted pie you want to make, use $1^3/4$ cups of unsifted flour, a dash of salt, $1/2$ cup plus 1 tablespoon of shortening or homemade lard (if you can get it from your butcher), and 6 to 9 tablespoons of ice water, using as little water as possible to make the dough. Put the flour and salt in a crock or ceramic bowl. (Mother made her piecrust in a pretty blue-and-white speckled dishpan that she didn't use for anything else.) Make a well in the flour and add the shortening. Mix the flour and shortening until it gets crumbly and looks like coarse meal. To do this you can use a pastry blender, two knives, or your fingers. (Mother and the farm women I know who have made five or six pies a week their whole lives just use their fingers. The motion is something like this: pretend you have something sticky like chewing gum on your thumb and you use your other four fingers to get it off. Personally I think this mixing gesture is the secret of piecrust. Don't work the dough any longer than necessary or it will get tough.) Next, drizzle the ice water over the crust, spoonful by spoonful, and blend it with a fork or your fingers until incorporated. If necessary, add more ice water, drop by drop, over the dry, loose crumbs until the dough forms a ball. Knead it a couple of times until it's smooth. Divide the dough into 2 pieces, one slightly larger than the other.

To roll out the dough, put the larger piece on a floured board. Dust your hands and the rolling pin with flour. A heavy, wooden rolling pin is very important; without one you'll never be able to get the weight necessary to make a thin crust. Form the dough into a perfect ball and flatten it with the heel of your hand. Then start using your rolling pin, working in every direction. Lightly flour the top of the dough and the rolling pin as necessary to keep it from sticking and make a circle that's at least 2 inches bigger than the pie pan all the way around. Gently pick up the crust and fit it in the pie pan. Start rolling out your top crust. If you have a very high filling, as you will with uncooked fruit, it must be at least 3 inches in diameter bigger than the bottom crust.

Pour the filling into the bottom crust and dot with butter. Place the top crust on the pie and pinch and flute the edges together. To flute, pinch the seams of the top and bottom crusts between your thumb and index finger, with your thumb slightly lower. Remember, there are three reasons why you flute: it's pretty; the edge keeps some of the juice from dripping over; and it makes it easier to cut the pie. Cut symmetrical slits in the top crust with a dull knife.

If you want a fully baked, single-crust pie shell, as you would for Fancy Fresh Strawberry Pie (page 34), make half of the recipe and do not divide the dough when you roll it out. Put the bottom crust in the pie pan and prick it full of holes with a fork to keep it from getting air pockets. Preheat the oven to 400° and bake the pie shell for about 10 minutes, or until lightly browned.

Here's a secret I learned from Mother for making a prebaked pie shell: turn a pie pan upside down and fit the dough over the outside of the bottom. Bake the crust on the bottom of the pan the same as you would if the crust were inside the pie pan. After it has cooled you can invert the pie shell onto a nice glass plate and just lift the pie pan away. The piecrust should be strong enough to hold the filling without breaking, but if it seems fragile, or if you have an especially heavy filling (like mincemeat, raisin, or fruit), just drop the shell into a slightly larger pie pan.

MOTHER'S FRESH STRAWBERRY PANCAKES

✦ Thinly slice enough fresh strawberries to measure 2 cups, then sweeten with ¼ cup of sugar and set aside for 15 minutes or so to form a syrup.

Preheat the pancake griddle. In a large pitcher, sift together 1 cup of whole wheat flour, 1 cup of unbleached white flour, 2½ teaspoons of baking powder, and a teaspoon of salt.

In a bowl, mix ⅓ cup of vegetable oil with 1½ cups of milk. (For a variation you can use sour milk, which you make simply by adding a little vinegar to whole milk or buttermilk. If you do, increase the milk by 2 tablespoons and add a teaspoon of baking soda to the batter.) Beat 2 whole eggs and add to the milk and oil. Quickly stir the liquids into the dry ingredients just until most of the lumps dissolve. Fold in the strawberries and, if you want, a handful of chopped walnuts. Thin the batter with milk as necessary until it's the consistency of a milk shake.

Pour out the pancakes and fry until bubbles form on the top and the edges start to brown. Flip and cook on the other side until done. Serve with hot maple syrup. Makes 16 to 18 pancakes.

This delicious fruit [the strawberry] is so easily
cultivated, so healthful, and so universally popular,
that it is worthwhile for every farmer to raise it in
quantities sufficient, at least, to supply his own family.

—The Farmer's Almanac (1872)

Leftovers to Treasure

A weed is no more than a flower in disguise . . .

—J. R. Lowell,
"A Fable for Critics"

With the exception of the last day of school, the most exciting time in the spring was when Grandpa or Daddy went to town to buy the seed for planting. Until I was about ten, most of my dresses were made from "feed sacks." These were big, one-hundred-pound bags used for seed or feed that were made of sweet cotton calico prints with white or blue backgrounds, red roses, peonies, or daisies. Certain grains were just too fine for burlap, so these more tightly-woven prints were used. Mother, like the other farmers' wives, encouraged her husband to buy the products that came in these pretty fabrics so we could use them for clothing. My favorite was a bright red plaid, which Sue, the seamstress in the family, made into an adorable jumper for me. In the third grade I cherished a brilliant yellow feed sack with indigo-blue morning glories that became a matching skirt and blouse.

Since I didn't have any younger sisters to give my hand-me-downs to and my cousins were too citified to wear them, Mamaw Tribby cut up my feed-sack dresses into quilt pieces. Years later, when I was in my early twenties, after Mother died, I was sorting through boxes of linens when I discovered the bright bits of cloth from my childhood. This was before the resurgence in quilting and I couldn't find anyone to make them up for me. A neighbor in Little Cincinnati, Ima Carmichael, had been a prize-winning quilt maker, but she was giving it up because it was hard on her eyes and fingers. Still, when I showed her the pieces and told her that Mamaw had saved them for me, she decided to make one last quilt. The pieces now form eight-point stars on a plain white background with tulips and squares quilted in white thread. Every time I look at my quilt, I remember how those feed sacks went from being stacked in a barn, to being a little girl's favorite new dress, to becoming a family treasure.

> *In the sky the bright stars glittered,*
> *On the bank the pale moon shone.*
> *And 'twas from Aunt Dinah's quilting party,*
> *I was seeing Nellie home.*

> —folk song, "The Quilting Party"

✦✦✦✦✦✦✦✦✦✦✦✦✦✦✦✦✦✦✦✦✦✦✦✦✦✦✦✦✦✦✦✦✦✦✦✦

*The first day of spring was once the time for
taking young virgins into the fields, there in dalliance
to set an example for Nature to follow. Now we just
set the clock an hour ahead and change the oil in the
crankcase.*

—E. B. White, "Hot Weather"

*In the upland hills of southern Indiana the old-timers, who passed the day
at the feed store whittling around the woodstove, were renowned for their
yarns. Sometimes, when he wasn't in a hurry, Grandpa would let me
go with him to buy feed. While he was doing business with Mr. Yoho,
I'd scrunch up between the burlap bags and listen. I heard them say
that in the old days the people from the hills of Missouri, the Ozarks,
cavorted naked in the fields on the tilled earth at the time of planting to
make the corn grow tall. This was, of course, before fertilizer. They swore
it was true.*

*A little Madness in the Spring
Is wholesome even for the King.*

—Emily Dickinson,
"No. 1333"

✦✦✦✦✦✦✦✦✦✦✦✦✦✦✦✦✦✦✦✦✦✦✦✦✦✦✦✦✦✦✦✦✦✦✦✦

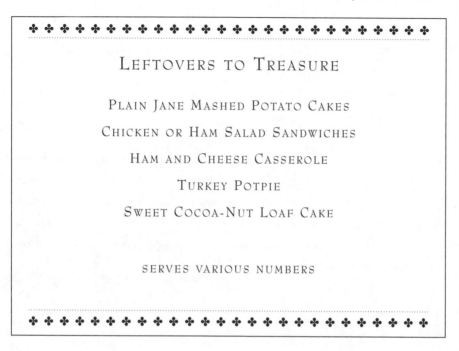

❖ ❖

LEFTOVERS TO TREASURE

PLAIN JANE MASHED POTATO CAKES

CHICKEN OR HAM SALAD SANDWICHES

HAM AND CHEESE CASSEROLE

TURKEY POTPIE

SWEET COCOA-NUT LOAF CAKE

SERVES VARIOUS NUMBERS

❖ ❖

PLAIN JANE MASHED POTATO CAKES

✦   Make 6 individual patties out of 3 cups of cold mashed potatoes. Coat each patty in flour. Season with salt and pepper. Fry in ¼ cup of hot vegetable oil in a cast-iron skillet until browned on both sides. Serves six.

CHICKEN OR HAM SALAD SANDWICHES

✦   Dice 2 cups of leftover chicken or ham into small cubes. Add a cup of finely chopped celery, 3 chopped hard-boiled eggs, 2 teaspoons of sweet relish, ¾ cup of mayonnaise, and salt and white pepper. If you are making chicken salad, season with a teaspoon of dill weed; with ham salad, I like to add a teaspoon of prepared mustard and a dash of vinegar. Chill.

For sandwiches, toast homemade white bread and spread with may-onnaise. Add pieces of pimento for ham salad. Makes about 6 sandwiches.

HAM AND CHEESE CASSEROLE

✦   Make a cheese sauce by stirring a cup of shredded cheddar cheese and ½ cup of half-and-half over low heat until the mixture is creamy. Take the pan off the heat and add about 2 cups of diced leftover ham, 2½ cups of cubed cooked potatoes, and 2 teaspoons of Worcestershire sauce. Stir well.

Pour the mixture into a casserole dish and bake for 45 minutes in a moderate (350°) oven. Serves six to eight.

TURKEY POTPIE

✦   Pull leftover turkey into equal pieces. In a Dutch oven melt 3 tablespoons of butter and sauté a chopped medium onion. Add 2 heaping tablespoons of flour, stir it, and let it cook briefly into the but-ter. Add 3 cups of milk and cook, stirring, to make a thin gravy. Mix the turkey into the gravy and season with salt, coarse-ground pepper, ½ teaspoon of rubbed sage, and a little paprika. Mix in a cup of water and let the turkey simmer over a very low heat for 20 to 30 minutes, or until it has made a thin gravy and the flavors are blended.

Stir in 2 to 4 cups of cooked vegetables. (Leftovers or frozen veg-etables are fine to use. If the vegetables haven't been cooked before, steam them first. Red peppers and broccoli add color to the dish, but green beans, potatoes, corn, mushrooms, and any other vegetables you have in the refrigerator are fine in any combination.) Pour into a casserole.

Prepare Buttermilk Stir-Up Biscuits (page 28) and put them, uncooked, on top of the turkey mixture. Bake in a hot (425°) oven for about 20 minutes, or until the biscuits are browned. Makes about 12 servings, one biscuit per person.

SWEET COCOA-NUT LOAF CAKE

✦ Sift together 2 cups of cake flour with 2 teaspoons of baking powder, 3 tablespoons of good baking cocoa, 1½ teaspoons of cinnamon, ¼ teaspoon of ground cloves, and ¼ teaspoon of nutmeg.

In another bowl, cream together ⅔ cup of butter and 2 cups of sugar. Beat 3 large eggs until they are foamy, add to the butter and sugar, and stir well. Fold in a cup of reheated mashed potatoes with a pinch of salt added. (If the potatoes have not been salted previously, use ½ teaspoon.) Stir a teaspoon of vanilla extract into ½ cup of milk.

Alternately blend the potato batter and vanilla milk with the sifted ingredients. Beat well. Stir in ¾ cup of chopped nuts. Spoon the batter into a greased 13-by-9-inch baking pan.

Bake in a preheated 325° oven for about 45 minutes, or until a toothpick or broom straw stuck in the middle comes out clean. Slice after cooling. Makes about 10 slices.

Turkey in the straw, turkey in the hay,
Roll 'em up and twist 'em up a high tuckahaw,
And hit 'em up a tune call Turkey in the Straw,

—folk song, "Turkey in the Straw"

SUMMER

Haying in the Fields, Canning in the Kitchen

Summer afternoon—summer afternoon; to me those have always been the two most beautiful words in the English language.

—Henry James,
as quoted by Edith Wharton

Mamaw Tribby's
Journal

*A*ll of her life, Mamaw Tribby—Bessie Collings Tribby—kept home-made journals and scrapbooks with cardboard covers tied with the same heavy thread she used to make braided rugs. During the winter, when she couldn't garden, she wrote stories and poetry about her memories and dreams. In 1920, the same year Grandpa Hutchens moved back to Greene County and began farming, Mamaw Tribby started a history of her husband's family. The last entry was dated November 4, 1955. As the story goes, this journal began when Emma Tribby Collins, one of the Ohio Tribbys, wrote to Mamaw asking for information about the Indiana Tribbys. The Tribby Family History, like all of her "books," was liberally sprinkled with family photographs, garden-ing ideas, and recipes—all the important aspects of her life. Although her formal education ended with the eighth grade, her books tell us about the joys and struggles of the everyday life of a farmer's wife in the early part of this century.

In the following pages from one of her journals, Mamaw Tribby describes Walnut Valley, the family homestead.

There's an old grapevine by the well
That's broken and needing care.
There's the cherry tree loaded with blossoms
And under it an old rocking chair...

June, 1938

In the year 1860 Michael Tribby, a shoemaker with only one leg (he lost the other from a case of typhoid fever), brought his family from Ohio to Solsberry, Indiana, where he built the old home place in a valley between two hills scattered with walnut trees. This was my father-in-law. My husband, William Henry, grew up in that large frame house with high ceilings, two fireplaces and two large old walnut cupboards with a snowball bush at one window and a red rambling rose at the other. An everlasting spring came out of the hill on the east side of the house with an old walnut shade tree beside it. I started living in Walnut Valley, for that's what we called it, in 1903, when I married William.

In the summer I did my washing under the old walnut tree

while the children played with their dog, Bruce. William would leave his log wagon in its shade when he would come in for the noon meal and let Nellie, his horse, drink the good cold water in the old watering trough fed by the spring. We had persimmons, gallons and gallons of blackberries, wild grapes, an orchard filled with cherries, peaches and pears and some of the best White Transparent and Maiden Blush as well as Grime's Golden and Early June apples you could ever imagine. Far away from the walnut trees, I always put out a good garden. Every year I had tomatoes, at least three kinds of beans--bunch, limas and pole--corn, squash, potatoes, cabbage, mangos and new peas. I usually tried something different, like cauliflower or musk melon to see if they could be cultivated and if the family would like them.

In this home there were births, deaths and marriages and the children played in the rippling waters of the branch. Those summer days were the happiest of my long life.

Bessie Tribby

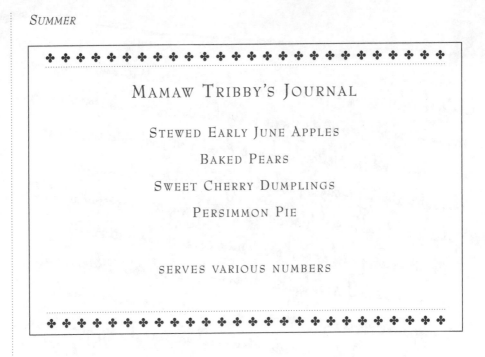

MAMAW TRIBBY'S JOURNAL

STEWED EARLY JUNE APPLES

BAKED PEARS

SWEET CHERRY DUMPLINGS

PERSIMMON PIE

SERVES VARIOUS NUMBERS

STEWED EARLY JUNE APPLES

✦   This is a wonderful, simple way to cook Early June apples, those that you see on roadsides all over the Midwest at the beginning of summer. (If you can't find Early June apples, you can substitute Granny Smiths, peeled.) These tiny, tart apples have a delicate skin so light they almost look white. Mamaw always cooked them with the skin.

Wash and slice 6 cups of apples. Melt 4 tablespoons of butter in a cast-iron skillet and put the apples in the hot pan. Add $1/2$ cup of sugar, a pinch of salt, and $1/2$ teaspoon of cinnamon. Cover and simmer over a low heat, stirring occasionally, until the apples are lightly browned and tender—10 to 15 minutes. Serve hot or cold with heavy cream or as a side dish with pork. Serves six.

BAKED PEARS

✦   Peel 7 large pears and cut in half. Rub lightly with lemon juice to keep from darkening. Hollow out the core and arrange cut sides up in a buttered baking dish. In a bowl, combine 1 cup of packed dark brown sugar, $1/2$ cup of small black walnut pieces, $1/4$ cup of flour, $1/2$ teaspoon of cinnamon, $1/2$ teaspoon of nutmeg, and a dash of ground cloves. Fill the hollows of the pears with a heaping spoonful of the filling and sprinkle the rest on top. Pour enough hot water in the pan to reach about a quarter of the way up the sides of the pears.

Bake in a preheated 350° oven for 25 minutes, or until tender when pierced with a fork. Baste the pears with the liquid once or twice while they bake. Serve warm. Makes 14 servings.

SWEET CHERRY DUMPLINGS

✦   Pit 5 cups of sweet cherries and put in a deep pot. Make a syrup of $1 1/2$ cups of sugar and 3 cups of boiling water and pour over the cherries. (Adjust the amount of sugar you use, based on the sweetness of the cherries.) Stir in $1/4$ teaspoon of almond extract. Cover, bring to a boil, and cook over a medium heat for about 5 minutes. Keep the syrup slowly boiling. Add a tablespoon of lemon juice. Dissolve 2 tablespoons of cornstarch in $1/4$ cup of cold water, stir into the cherries, and cook, stirring until slightly thickened.

To make dumplings, sift together $1 1/2$ cups of unbleached flour, 2 teaspoons of baking powder, and $1/2$ cup of sugar. Add $3/4$ teaspoon of salt and $3/4$ cup of milk and mix well. If it is too dry to incorporate all of the flour, add more milk, drop by drop, until the batter is soft and sticky. Don't stir more than necessary. Knead the batter a couple of times in the bowl.

Drop the dumpling batter, a heaping tablespoonful at a time, into the simmering cherries. (If you keep dipping the spoon in hot water, the dough will not stick to it as much.) Cover the pot and simmer over a low heat for about 15 minutes. Use a fork to test one of the dumplings to make sure that it is no longer "doughy." Try not to overlap the dumplings, so that they don't stick together. Makes 12 to 14 dumplings. Serve each person a couple of dumplings with plenty of syrup and cherries. Sweet Cherry Dumplings are delicious warm or cold, with milk, sweetened whipped cream, or plain. Serves six to seven.

> *Davy, Davy Dumpling*
> *Boil him in the pot;*
> *Sugar him and butter him,*
> *And eat him while he's hot.*

> —nursery rhyme

PERSIMMON PIE

✦ Remove the skins from persimmons and mash enough to make 1 cup of pulp. If you use wild persimmons, you will need to start with about a quart (or 20), and you should rub them through a colander. Cultivated persimmons can just be mashed by hand. Cultivated persimmons are also larger—you will need only about 6 of them, depending on their size. Make sure that they are *very* ripe.

Add to the pulp 1 cup of sugar, ³/₄ teaspoon of cinnamon, a dash of salt and nutmeg, and 2 beaten egg yolks. Mix thoroughly, and then stir in a cup of milk. Whip 2 egg whites until they are stiff and fold into the persimmon batter.

Pour the batter into an unbaked piecrust (see page 34); do not cover with a top crust. Bake in a preheated 450° oven for 10 minutes.

Reduce the heat to 350° and bake for another 45 minutes, or until firm. A knife stuck in the center of the pie should come out clean.

+ +

The flowers are of all heights. . . . But there is no crushing or
crowding. Each individual has room to display its full perfection.
                                    —Celia Thaxter, *An Island Garden*

From Mamaw Tribby I learned to love random variety in a garden—
down-home black-eyed Susans next to wispy, deep-pink cosmos, scat-
tered among whatever seeds she had left over or perennials that had
already staked their claim. She called gardens that were filled with long
rows of one kind of flower "armies."

*   "People are like plants, they don't flourish unless we let them*
be themselves," she would say when we went out for a drive and
passed a house that had an army in the front yard.

+ +

In an orchard there should be enough to eat,
enough to lay up,
enough to be stolen,
and enough to rot upon the ground.

                                        —Samuel Johnson (1783)

A Hay Hands' Feast

From the fields there comes the breath of new-mown hay;
Through the sycamores the candle lights are gleaming
On the banks of the Wabash, far away.

—Paul Dresser,
    "On the Banks of the Wabash"

"Make hay while the sun shines," Daddy would say every morning when it was haying time as he silently willed the hot, dry weather to hold out until they were finished. Before sunrise his voice boomed from the bottom of the stairs, "Rise and shine, this ain't paying the preacher." He had the bacon spitting and crackling and the coffee perking before I wandered down to the kitchen to finish up breakfast. By the time Daddy and my brothers had grabbed their caps with the Pioneer seed corn insignia, the young men hired as hay hands were on the back porch ready to get started. Mother and I watched them head out for the first load and then went inside to start the bread.

Everybody understood that you fed hay hands with as fine a noon meal as you could put together. Each day for the week they were working in hay we made a dinner with at least two main dishes, several desserts, homemade bread, mashed potatoes and gravy, three or four other vegetables, and some salads. Right after we set the bread to rise in the sun on the back porch swing, we made up the pies and cobblers so we wouldn't have to heat the oven during the hottest part of the day. Using the rolling pin that Mamaw Tribby had given her when she got married, Mother made perfect circles of dough for the bottom crust and cut strips to basket-weave the lattice tops, while I sweetened and spiced mounds of peaches, apples, or berries to fill the pies. Then Mother and I would sit a minute with a cup of coffee to catch our breath before I'd clean up all the flour from the baking. While I peeled potatoes and began the rest of the meal, Mother started the other chores, which didn't stop just because we were in hay.

By noon the table was set, the vegetables were served, the rolls were just ready to come out of the oven, and I was about to mash the potatoes. The wagons clattered up the lane and pulled into the barn lot, while the voices of hungry young men floated in through the windows. No matter what else needed to be done, I'd run into the bathroom and put on some lipstick and comb my hair before I'd let every fellow in eastern Greene County see me with flour on my face.

Ready to go back to the hayfield as soon as the hands finish lunch.

We had basins set up under the trees with plenty of hot water and Boraxo for the hands to wash up before they came into our clean kitchen. I'd wander outside to visit for a minute—just to be friendly. Then all of them would squeeze around Mother's big kitchen table, which seated fourteen if we used all its leaves. There was never enough room for anything but yeast rolls and homemade butter on the table, so we set up the hot food and desserts on the counter like a sideboard. Mother and I stood in the kitchen and talked to the men as we poured iced tea and handed them the dishes for seconds and thirds. After they ate, we sat down and put our feet up, ate what was left, and figured out what we were going to make the next day.

The big doors of the country barn stand open and ready,
The dried grass of the harvest time loads the slow-drawn wagon. . . .
I jump from the crossbeams and seize the clover and timothy,
And roll head over heels and tangle my hair full of wisps.

—Walt Whitman, "Song of Myself"

A HAY HANDS' FEAST

MOIST AND CRUNCHY FRIED CHICKEN AND GRAVY

AUNT ESTHER'S MEAT LOAF

SLIGHTLY LUMPY MASHED POTATOES

FRIED CORN

GREEN BEANS, COUNTRY STYLE

MOTHER'S SPECIAL YEAST ROLLS

MAMAW HUTCHENS' ONE-CRUST RASPBERRY COBBLER

"GET YOU A BOYFRIEND" PEACH PIE

SERVES VARIOUS NUMBERS

MOIST AND CRUNCHY FRIED CHICKEN AND GRAVY

✦ Wash and dry 3 large (3 to 4 pounds each) cut-up fryers. Salt and pepper the chicken pieces. Stir 3 eggs into 2 cups of milk and blend. Dip the chicken, one piece at a time, into this mixture, then dredge it in flour until well-coated. (We usually fried chicken in two big electric skillets to keep the stove free when we were cooking for hay hands, but when cooking in smaller quantities, use a cast-iron skillet.)

Melt about a cup of vegetable shortening in each skillet and add 3 to 4 tablespoons of bacon fat. When the fat is hot, add the chicken and quickly brown on all sides, using high heat. After the pieces turn dark brown, cover the skillet and cook over a very low heat for about 45 minutes, or until done. While it's cooking, sprinkle a little water on the chicken, but don't lift the lid more than necessary. (This allows the chicken to steam and makes it moist on the inside with a hard, nutty crust.)

When the chicken is done, let it drain on paper towels. Keep the skillets hot. In each skillet add about 7 tablespoons of flour to the drippings and stir until the lumps cook out. You should have about equal amounts of drippings and flour. Add a quart of milk to each skillet. Turn the heat down to a simmer and stir continuously until the gravy is the consistency of a milk shake. Sprinkle on salt and pepper to taste. Of course, you'll serve the gravy over ever-so-slightly lumpy mashed potatoes. This will make 2 quarts of gravy. Serves fourteen.

AUNT ESTHER'S MEAT LOAF

✦   Mother's baby sister, Esther, was the aunt I could always count on to defend me when my brothers or cousins were getting the upper hand. This meat loaf was her specialty and she taught me to make it when I was first learning how to cook.

Make a sauce for the meat loaf by heating 2 cups of packed, dark-brown sugar with ³/₄ cup of water, 1¹/₂ tablespoons of prepared mustard, and ³/₄ cup of apple cider vinegar. Cook over a medium heat until the sauce is well mixed and comes to a boil. Turn off the heat.

Mix 3 pounds of ground round or chuck and 1 pound of pork sausage (see the recipe on page 26) in a large bowl. Add a finely chopped large onion, 1 tablespoon of salt, $^1/_4$ teaspoon of coarsely ground black pepper, 3 slightly beaten eggs, a cup of ketchup, 2 cups of cracker crumbs, and $^1/_2$ cup of milk. Mix with your hands until the meat sticks together in a mass. If it is too loose, gradually add more cracker crumbs; if it is too dry, gradually add more ketchup.

Divide the meat mixture in half. Form each half into a loaf about 5 inches wide and place each in the middle of a 10-inch cast-iron skillet. Pour half of the sauce over each meat loaf. Use a pastry brush or spoon to coat the whole loaf, so it runs down the sides and covers the bottom of the skillet.

Bake the meat loaves uncovered in a preheated 400° oven for 45 to 60 minutes, or until very dark brown. Baste the meat loaves with the sauce a couple of times during the baking. Makes 14 to 16 servings.

SLIGHTLY LUMPY MASHED POTATOES

✦   In our neck of the woods, potatoes were taken very seriously; you wouldn't wish a bad potato crop on your worst enemy.

Just about everybody thinks that the way their family makes mashed potatoes is the best way and has a family secret to explain their success. Maybe that's the way it should be. Not to be outdone, I want to let you in on our family's secret.

Peel 2 dozen russet potatoes (I always use $1^1/_2$ medium potatoes per person) and cut into pieces. Put them in a large kettle with salted water and bring to a boil. Cook for 20 to 30 minutes, or until they are tender when stuck with a fork. Drain off the water and transfer the potatoes to a big mixing bowl.

Heat a cup of butter, a cup of half-and-half, and $^1/_3$ cup of milk in a saucepan until the butter begins to get soft and the liquids are a little warmer than room temperature. Meanwhile, start whipping the potatoes with a hand masher. (Potatoes mashed with an electric mixer really do taste different.) When they are halfway mashed, pour in half of the liquid and the butter and add salt. Continue mashing until you've incorporated the liquid, and then, as you continue to mash, gradually add the rest, a little at a time. Stop adding liquid and mashing when the overall consistency is smooth and firm but little lumps still pop out. Turn out into a big serving bowl and dot the top with more butter and a sprinkle of coarse-ground black pepper. Makes about 16 servings.

Fried Corn

✦   Even when they are on their best behavior, hay hands are usually a little messy. Corn on the cob was always one of their favorites but for the next several days we would find little corn kernels lodged in the corners of the kitchen. Mother's solution was to cut the corn off the cob and fry it.

Shuck and remove the silk from about 2 dozen ears of corn (about 2 ears per person). Hold each ear on one end with the other end balanced in a flat pan and cut off the corn kernels as close to the cob as possible. Rotate the ear as you cut. Scrape the back of the knife blade over the cobs to draw out the milk.

In a large cast-iron skillet, melt $1/2$ cup of butter over a medium heat. Add the corn, salt, pepper, 2 tablespoons of sugar, and $1/2$ cup of cream. (According to Mamaw Hutchens, the sugar is the most important ingredient because it brings out the natural sweetness of the corn.) Fry the corn, stirring frequently, for 15 to 20 minutes, or until the corn is tender but not mushy. Makes about 24 average servings.

This is a great way to enjoy fresh corn at the end of the season, when it's getting too tough on the cob for even the most confirmed corn fanatic.

GREEN BEANS, COUNTRY STYLE

✦   People today have such strong feelings about vegetables not being cooked too long that it's hard to get anyone to believe how special this dish is. We enjoyed Green Beans, Country Style, year-round thanks to home-canned green beans (see page 70). It's one of the specialties we inherited from the southern pioneers, and it means "home" to anyone who grew up on a midwestern farm.

Break off the ends and string 4 pounds of fresh-picked green beans. Wash and break them into 2-inch pieces. Slowly fry 6 pieces of bacon in the bottom of a Dutch oven. When the bacon is almost cooked, add the beans and stir constantly for 5 minutes. Add 1 cup of water. Turn down the heat, cover the kettle, and cook very slowly, without lifting the lid, for an hour. The beans should "cook down" until fully cooked and flattened out. (Make sure they don't burn, but don't add more liquid than necessary to keep them from burning; they should be cooked almost dry when they are finished.)

For a variation, you can add several small boiling onions or substitute ham or salt pork for the bacon. Also, you can make a large batch and they will be delicious for several days. Makes 16 servings.

MOTHER'S SPECIAL YEAST ROLLS

✦   Mother made many kinds of homemade breads, but when we had company—and hay hands were considered company—she took out her blue earthenware bowl and made these rolls.

Scald 2 cups of milk (heat until a skim forms on the top but do not boil). Add ¼ cup of sugar, 2 teaspoons of salt, and 4 tablespoons of margarine to the milk. Set the mixture aside in a large mixing bowl to cool to lukewarm.

Dissolve 2 tablespoons of active dry yeast in ½ cup of lukewarm water. Add this to the milk mixture (don't do this while the milk is still hot or it will kill the yeast). Start adding unbleached white flour in small amounts, stirring well, and keep adding flour and stirring until the dough pulls away from the sides of the bowl. I like to knead in the bowl and then turn out the dough onto a floured board. Continue adding flour and kneading until the dough has a puffy, elastic look; you should knead for approximately 300 turns. You'll need 6 to 7 cups of flour in all.

Place the dough in a greased bowl and turn it so the greased side is up. Cover with a damp cloth. Let it rise in a warm spot until it doubles in bulk, 45 minutes or an hour.

Punch down the dough by pushing your fist in as far as it will go. Turn the dough over and let it rise again until doubled, 20 to 30 minutes.

Punch down the dough again. Make it into rolls by pinching off a ball of dough about the size of a small egg. With the heel of your hand, flatten each ball into a 2-inch circle that's about $1/2$ inch thick. Gather the outside edges of the circle together as if forming a small bag. Twist the top closed and push it down into the dough. Put the rolls, 1 to 2 inches apart, smooth sides up, on a greased baking sheet. Let rise until doubled, 30 to 45 minutes.

Bake in a preheated 400° oven until the rolls are browned, about 15 minutes. Makes 25 to 30 rolls.

MAMAW HUTCHENS' ONE-CRUST RASPBERRY COBBLER

✦   When Grandpa was only forty-six years old, my Grandmother Flo passed away. In those days—and especially in rural areas—marriage was based on practical considerations as well as romance. A farm really couldn't get along without a woman to garden, can, and cook. Grandpa was lucky to find Mamaw Dess. A funny, wonderful woman who could cook rings around most fancy chefs, she was a widow with four kids who needed a home and father. Almost every day after school, I'd go visit with her and see if she had a cobbler in the oven. This is the way she made it.

Grease a 13-by-9-inch baking dish with butter. In a mixing bowl, combine 6 cups of washed and drained raspberries with 2 cups of sugar, $2/3$ cup of flour, and 1 teaspoon of cinnamon and nutmeg mixed together. Taste it to make sure it's sweet enough; if it isn't, add more sugar. (Raspberries can be very tart. Nothing is more upsetting for a baker than having the first person who takes a big bite out of your beautiful fresh raspberry cobbler make a face because it's too sour!) Spread the fruit mixture over the bottom of the baking dish and dot the top with butter.

Make enough pastry for a single-crust pie (see page 35). Roll or pat out the crust to match the shape of the baking dish, lay it on top of the fruit, and cut several slits in the top for juice to seep out. Sprinkle a teaspoon of sugar and a little cinnamon on the crust.

Bake in a preheated 350° oven until browned on top, 25 to 30 minutes. As you would expect, this bakes faster than a pie because it's only a top crust. Makes 15 servings.

"GET YOU A BOYFRIEND" PEACH PIE

✦ While we were cooking, Mother used to tease me that my peach pie would surely get me a date with one of the hay hands to go to the Greene County Fair. Once in a while it did. We always liked the Belle of Georgia variety but just about any fresh, ripe peach makes a wonderful pie.

Peel and slice enough fresh ripe peaches to measure 5 cups. Add $3/4$ cup of sugar, $1/3$ cup of flour, $1/2$ teaspoon of cinnamon, a pinch of ground cardamom, and a teaspoon of lemon juice. Stir well.

Pour into an unbaked 9-inch pie shell (see page 34) and dot the top with 1 tablespoon of butter. Top with a solid or lattice-weaved crust.

Bake in a preheated hot (425°) oven until browned, about 35 minutes.

Dandelion Dreams

Four dandelion blossoms.
  That is all that they are.
But to me they were sweeter
  Than roses by far.
The stems are too short
  Of that I'm aware.
And, the blossoms are wilted
  But, what do I care.
She gave them to me.
  They were wet with the dew.
And she whispered,
  Here, Mom, some flowers for you.

—Mamaw Tribby,
  poem for Veva,
  my mother (June 1925)

Mamaw Tribby and I spent a lot of time talking about weeds because we spent a lot of time pulling them. Even though she could happily cook up a mess of dandelions for a light supper, she hated them when they got into her flowers. Every time she found a dandelion, you'd hear a squeal of triumph as she carefully pulled it up by the roots. A dandelion in a garden, she explained, is just like deceit among friends: you don't always see it until it blooms, but then you better pull it out by the roots or it will multiply.

I used to love my garden,
But now my love is dead,
For I found a bachelor's button
In black-eyed Susan's bed.

—Source unknown

Dandelion Salad

✦   Wash, drain, and dry about 2 quarts of young dandelion greens with small leaves and no flower buds; cut into 2-inch strips and put in a salad bowl.

Fry 1/4 pound of bacon until it's crisp; pour the fat and bacon over the dandelion greens. Melt 1 tablespoon of butter in the skillet and add 1/4 cup of heavy cream. Beat an egg and add it to the butter and cream along with 1 teaspoon of salt, 1/4 teaspoon of pepper, and 2 tablespoons of sugar (or to taste). Simmer over a very low heat, stirring constantly until the dressing is heated through and begins to thicken. Drizzle over the greens and toss well. Makes 8 servings.

◆ ◆

Many eyes go through the meadow, but few see the flowers.
—English proverb

When he was working in his garden, the man who lived across the road from Mamaw Tribby used to cuss and shake his fist like he was being attacked by enemy soldiers. When the wind was blowing in our direction, we could hear his rantings and ravings, but it was never over anything that amounted to a hill of beans. This upset Mamaw Tribby, who believed that plants were sensitive and could be hurt as easily as people. She was always preaching to me that you had to be extra careful how you treated plants because they couldn't talk or strike back. Without even looking up, Mamaw Tribby would mutter under her breath, "People show their true colors when they work in the garden."

A bad gardener quarrels with his rake.
—American proverb

◆ ◆

Putting It Away for Winter

All my bones were made of Indian corn.
Delicious grain! whatever form it take,
To roast or boil, to smother or to bake . . .
    Let the green succotash with thee contend,
Let beans and corn their sweetest juices blend,
Let butter drench them in its yellow tide,
And a long slice of bacon grace their side . . .

—Joel Barlow,
    "The Hasty Pudding"

When the green beans, corn, tomatoes, or cucumbers were ripe in the garden, it was time to can as much as we could for winter. By the end of summer, the shelves of the basement would be filled with hundreds of mason jars full of homemade jellies, fruit butters, bread-and-butter pickles, corn relishes, tomatoes and tomato juice, corn (before we got a deep-freeze), and an assortment of whatever Daddy felt like trying his hand at that summer. But the winter's mainstay was green beans, and we would "put away" over a hundred quarts of them.

Daddy was the one who determined exactly when a vegetable was at its peak, and then the women geared up for action. My sister Sue washed and sterilized the empty mason jars that we reused every year, while Mother and I were out in the garden right after sunrise, picking tomatoes or cucumbers or corn. After the dew had dried, we'd be out raking over long rows of green beans to fill bushel baskets. We congregated on the back porch, where it was a lot cooler than the kitchen. Surrounded by produce, we sat in the swing or on the floor with our laps full of beans to break or corn to husk. And then we'd all fall into the bean-breaking song . . .

> Break both ends and throw them away,
> > snap, snap, snap, don't let the good ones go astray.
> Break both ends and throw them away,
> > snap, snap, snap, don't let the good ones go astray.

And on and on.

Sometimes my aunts or one of the neighbors helped us while we broke beans for hours. I loved their stories about the old days, the bluegrass songs and endless sentimental poems. Our favorite song was "Old Shep," about a dog who can't go on living after his master dies, and the poem, "The Little Match Girl," who froze to death because she didn't have the money to buy wood to keep warm. By the end of the day each of us had teared up at least once.

Lovely! See the cloud, the cloud appear!
Lovely! See the rain, the rain draw near!
Who spoke?
It was the little corn ear
High up on the tip of the stalk.

—Zuni song

When we needed rain on the farm and the plants seemed to wilt before
our eyes, I remember Daddy gazing out over the garden and the long
stretches of corn and wheat fields from a tiny window in the living room.
He would always do this after the noon meal—not saying a word and
standing for such a long time it seemed an eternity. I wanted to ask him
if everything would be all right. Would we have crops? Would we have

green beans, tomatoes, and corn
to put away for the winter? But
his silence and the furrow in his
brow were answer enough: he didn't
know. How much easier those times
would have been if we could have
performed a rain dance.

O farmers, pray that your summers be wet
    and your winters clear.

—Virgil

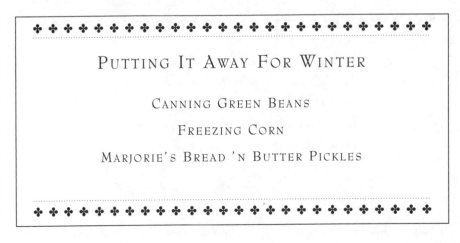

PUTTING IT AWAY FOR WINTER

CANNING GREEN BEANS

FREEZING CORN

MARJORIE'S BREAD 'N BUTTER PICKLES

CANNING GREEN BEANS

✦   We always canned green beans in a pressure canner using the hot-pack method: that means that they are parboiled before packing in the jars. Unless you have a pressure canner, vegetables, other than tomatoes, should be frozen, because of their low acid content. If you haven't canned before, contact your local extension agency of the United States Department of Agriculture for guidelines. They are very thorough and have a lot of information specifically for your geographical area.

In small batches, wash 2 pounds of beans for every quart you want to can. Break the beans into 1-inch pieces, carefully removing the tips and any bad spots. Make sure you use 1-quart, heat-tempered, standard mason jars that aren't cracked or nicked, especially around the rim where the seal fits. We bought new lids each year but reused screw bands if they were in perfect condition. Wash the jars, lids, and screw bands in very hot, soapy water and rinse well. Leave some hot water in the jars to keep them warm. This prevents breakage from quick changes in temperature.

Submerge the beans in boiling water for 3 minutes. (This preshrinks the beans so the jars pack fuller, and also guards against spoilage.)

Take a clean jar, discard the hot water in it, and pack it *loosely* with the parboiled beans. Add 1 teaspoon of salt or to taste. Fill the jar with the boiling liquid used to parboil the beans or with fresh boiling water, leaving about $1/2$ inch of head space at the top. Skim off the air bubbles and wipe the sealing edge clean. I use self-sealing flat lids with screw-on metal bands. Put the scalded, flat lid with the sealing compound on the sealing edge of the jar. Secure it by screwing on a metal band until the self-sealing is complete. The metal band should be tightly screwed on by hand. Self-sealing takes place as the jar cools.

Place the jars on the rack of a pressure canner filled with the amount of water recommended by the manufacturer, usually 2 to 3 inches. Follow the specific instructions accompanying your pressure canner, but generally, at less than 2,000 feet above sea level, process at 10 pounds of pressure for 25 minutes to can quarts, or 20 minutes for pints. Make sure you don't pack the jars too tightly in the canner. Put it on high heat and lock the cover in place. Allow steam to escape by opening the vent. After 10 minutes, close the vent and let the pressure rise to 10 pounds and start timing. Adjust the heat to keep the presure at 10 pounds during the entire 25 minutes.

Remove the canner from the heat and let the pressure decrease all the way to zero before you attempt to take the lid off. When the pressure reads zero, open the vent (it should not release any steam), remove the jars, and allow them to cool to room temperature. Leave

the metal bands on for at least 12 hours. When they are removed, the lids should be depressed. Check carefully. If they aren't, the contents must be treated as fresh food.

Ah! Few things are more satisfying than having a kitchen counter full of freshly canned green beans to put up for the winter.

What shall I learn of beans or beans of me? I cherish them, I hoe them, early and late I have an eye to them; and this is my day's work.

—Henry David Thoreau, *Walden*

FREEZING CORN

✦   Having fresh corn in the freezer is the next best thing to July. Corn is so easy to freeze and maintains its flavor so amazingly well, you'll start growing corn just to freeze it.

Freeze corn when it is perfect for eating—that means when you squeeze a kernel with your fingernail and juice squirts out. Approximately 2 large ears will make 1 pint for the freezer. Pick the corn just before you need it, shuck it, and carefully remove all silk. Blanch up to a dozen ears at a time for $4^1/_2$ minutes in a covered 3-to-4-gallon kettle filled with water. Drain the corn and immediately cool under cold running water.

Cut the kernels off the cobs as you would do for Fried Corn (see page 60), being careful not to include any bad spots. Scrape as much milk out of the cobs as possible. Mix the corn to insure consistency of texture and kernel size.

Spoon the corn into pint-size plastic freezer bags or rigid plastic freezer containers. Use only products that are made for the freezer. Squeeze out the air and seal. Freeze until you're ready to use.

MARJORIE'S BREAD 'N BUTTER PICKLES

✦   This is the way Mother's good friend, Marjorie Frye, made her wonderful crisp and crunchy pickles.

Wash $5\frac{1}{2}$ to 6 pounds of unpeeled pickling cucumbers and slice them crosswise, as thin as you can; don't use the ends or any bad spots. In a big pot, mix 6 large, white, thinly sliced onions with the cucumber slices; add $\frac{1}{2}$ cup of coarse, noniodized salt and cover with cold water. Cover with a tight lid and refrigerate for 3 hours, or until the cucumbers and onions are thoroughly chilled. (Sometimes people plant 2 or 3 trays of ice cubes in the cucumbers and onions as a way to make them crisper.) Drain.

In a $1\frac{1}{2}$-gallon stainless-steel pot, combine 4 cups of sugar, $1\frac{1}{2}$ teaspoons of turmeric, $1\frac{1}{2}$ teaspoons of mustard seeds, and 5 cups of white (5-percent acid) pickling vinegar. Add the drained cucumbers and onions. Slowly bring to a boil over a low heat. As soon as the mixture comes to a boil, spoon the pickles into sterilized 1-pint canning jars and add enough of the liquid to reach $\frac{1}{2}$ inch from the top rim. Wipe the rim, set the lid in place, and seal tight.

Process using the boiling-water canning method, following the United States Department of Agriculture Guidelines. If you are canning at an altitude of less than one thousand feet, process for 10 minutes, timing from when you place the jars in the hot water. Makes about 8 pints.

Chicken for Sunday Dinner

A man may work from sun to sun,
But a woman's work is never done.

—Anonymous

*B*y the time I was born, Grandpa had quit poultry farming and we kept just enough chickens for our own use. Along with fruits and vegetables, we canned thirty to forty quarts of chicken meat and broth for the winter. When you'd look out the window on a cold winter day and see company drive up unexpectedly, about the only special dish you could make at the drop of a hat was chicken and dumplings.

Killing chickens was women's work, but nobody really liked doing it because it was such a mess, with blood and feathers flying everywhere. Daddy still fed them most of the time, and Alan and I gathered the eggs. Sue, Alan, Jeff, and I all helped Mother as much as we could. We set up boards on sawhorses to make long wooden tables in the side yard between the house and the barn and rushed big pots filled with boiling water outside. Mother actually did the killing—she said it was too hard on children.

The first big job was just getting the chicken from the henhouse into the yard. We didn't know whether to laugh or cry as Mother carried some fat old bird feet first across the barnyard. As it twitched and danced around for dear life, we couldn't help thinking it knew exactly what was in store for it. As soon as she put it down to catch her breath, it took off like a lightning bolt. The younger hens that were not too fat to run would give all four of us a good chase before we caught them. Mother cut off their necks, and for a few seconds that seemed to last forever, they ran around, their wings flapping just like the saying goes. After they finally quit, we plucked them, doused them in hot water, and then "dressed" them.

We ate the young ones fresh, cut up and fried, moist and tender on the inside with a hard crunchy brown crust on the outside. The old ones were stewed until the meat fell off the bones and floated in the rich broth filled with millions of circles of yellow fat. This was what we canned. On Sundays, Mother would come home from church, put an apron over her good dress, and dust up the flour board to make dumplings or noodles to cook in the chicken meat and broth. We didn't give a thought to those summer days when we had killed the old hen.

✦ ✦

"Probably poultry has made me the most money during the past eleven years," Harlan Hutchens says. *"It has not only provided a steady income but has been an important fact in building up the fertility of the soil as poultry manure has been scattered over nearly every field."*

The poultry house which he has recently constructed is unique. He wanted to build it 20 feet wide by 120 feet long, but he did not have enough level ground. . . . But his experience in railroad shops had not been for naught. He conceived the idea of building the house in two 20 by 60-feet sections, placing one right in front of the other in saw-tooth fashion, much as many industrial shops are built. . . . He has also found this house to be a timesaver. For instance in gathering eggs, if he had to go down one big long poultry house, he would be 120 feet away when he got through. As it is, he simply goes in at one door, gathers the eggs in that section, passes over to the other side and returns gathering the eggs as he comes and ends up at the same end of the house which he entered. Many similar labor saving instances are told by him.

Mr. Hutchens maintains a flock of about 800 English-strain White Leghorns. He sells his eggs locally . . . and according to the records of the County Agriculture Agent, V.D. Sexon, . . . he has the largest return of any of the poultry raisers in the county. He feeds practically all home-grown feeds, the laying hens getting corn and sometimes wheat for scratch grain and a mash composed of 400 mixed feed and 100 pounds meat scraps.

About 1,000 baby chicks are bought every spring, though he has started as many as 2,000. They are put in clean brooder houses on clean ground. From these chicks about 400 pullets are saved and he continually culls out his hens in the spring and summer until he has only about 400 of them left. Then he starts the laying season with 800 in his flock.

—from the article "Hutchens Succeeds on Hills,"
by Lewis P. East (*The Indiana Farmers Guide,* June 27, 1931)

✦ ✦

I want there to be no peasant in my realm so poor that he will not have a chicken in his pot every Sunday.

—attributed to King Henry IV of France

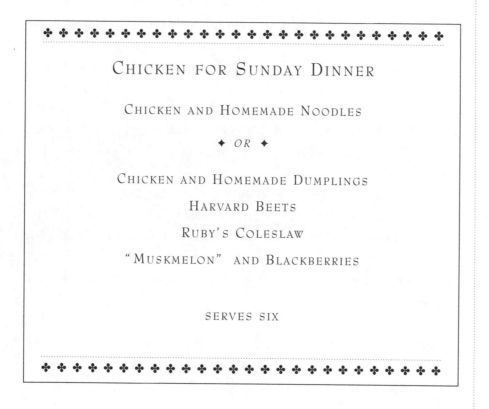

✤ ✤

CHICKEN FOR SUNDAY DINNER

CHICKEN AND HOMEMADE NOODLES

✦ *OR* ✦

CHICKEN AND HOMEMADE DUMPLINGS

HARVARD BEETS

RUBY'S COLESLAW

"MUSKMELON" AND BLACKBERRIES

SERVES SIX

✤ ✤

CHICKEN AND HOMEMADE NOODLES

✦   Boil a 5-to-6-pound stewing chicken in a large cast-iron kettle ²/₃ full of water. Add a bay leaf and salt and pepper. Simmer until tender and the meat begins to fall off the bones—2 to 3 hours.

Remove the chicken and skim the fat off the broth.

To make the noodles, beat 2 eggs. (One egg makes enough for

about 4 servings.) For each egg, add ¹/₂ an eggshell full of half-and-half. Add ¹/₂ teaspoon of salt (about ¹/₄ teaspoon for each egg). Sift in enough flour to make a stiff dough (about 1 cup) and knead on a floured board for a few turns. The dough will be stiffer and less oily than piecrust.

Using a rolling pin, roll out the dough into a rectangle until it is almost paper-thin. Sprinkle a couple of tablespoons of flour on the dough; cut into narrow strips (about ¹/₄ inch wide) using a sharp knife. Sprinkle with a little more flour and toss them lightly for a minute to let dry.

Bring the chicken broth to a boil. Add the noodles and cook until done—6 to 10 minutes. (Sometimes homemade noodles can be tough and require longer cooking time. Just simmer the noodles over low heat until they are tender.)

Add any small, loose pieces of chicken meat to the noodles and serve in a large bowl. Serve the large chicken pieces on a platter. The noodles are best with Slightly Lumpy Mashed Potatoes (see page 59). Makes about 3 cups of uncooked noodles. Extra uncooked noodles will keep for several weeks in the freezer. Store in plastic bags made for the freezer.

CHICKEN AND HOMEMADE DUMPLINGS

✦ Prepare the chicken the same as for the noodles.

To make dumplings, combine 1³/₄ cups of unsifted flour, 2 teaspoons of baking powder, and ¹/₂ teaspoon of salt in a mixing bowl. Add ³/₄ cup of milk, a slightly beaten jumbo egg, and 2 tablespoons of melted butter. Stir until the ingredients are evenly moistened.

Drop the dumplings by spoonfuls into the boiling chicken broth. Cook uncovered for about 10 minutes. Cover and cook over a low heat for another 5 to 10 minutes, or until the dumplings are no longer doughy. The dumplings should be served the same way as the noodles.

Oh, we'll all have chicken and dumplin's when she comes,
Oh, we'll all have chicken and dumplin's when she comes,
Oh, we'll all have chicken and dumplin's,
Oh, we'll all have chicken and dumplin's,
Oh, we'll all have chicken and dumplin's when she comes.

—folk song, "She'll Be Coming Around the Mountain"

HARVARD BEETS

✦ Beets are wonderful vegetables that don't get the attention they deserve. Delicious and very good for your liver—at least that's what Mamaw Tribby said!—they add a wonderful splash of color to otherwise bland-looking meals.

Wash 6 medium-size fresh beets and cut off their tops, leaving about 2 inches of the stem. Leave on the skins and the root tip. Place the beets in a saucepan with enough water to cover the tops by 1 inch; bring to a boil. Reduce the heat and simmer until tender—20 to 25 minutes. Remove the beets from the water and let them cool. Keep the cooking water for the sauce.

Peel the beets by just squeezing the skins: if they're done, they'll come right off. Cut the beets into 1/4-inch slices and set aside.

Make a sauce by combining 2 cups of the beet water, 1/4 cup of cider vinegar, 1/2 cup of sugar, and 1 teaspoon of salt in a stainless-steel saucepan. Stir and bring the mixture to a boil. Reduce the heat to low and prepare a mixture of 1/4 cup of cornstarch blended into 1/2 cup of cold water; add this to the sauce and stir until thickened to the consistency of chicken gravy. Add the beet slices and heat through, stirring all the while.

RUBY'S COLESLAW

✦   When I was twenty-five years old, Mother passed away after a ten-year fight against breast cancer. This was a sad but special time in our lives because Mother was so determined to savor every moment. She used to tell us not to feel sad, because she was going to get all of her living done in whatever time she had left and we had better do the same thing. Looking back on it, I think we all did. Sue gave Mother her first grandchildren, Philip and Alison, and Mother worshiped them. Alan and I both married and she helped each of us start our first homes. Just before she died, Alan's first child, blond, blue-eyed Michael Hutchens, was born. Still a teenager, Jeff was too young to lose his mother and received as much nurturing as all of us could give. Through all of this Daddy was always there in his own quiet way.

Several years later when Daddy remarried, all of us were very happy for him and for ourselves. His new wife, Ruby Weaver, a long-time neighbor and friend, welcomed us alongside the Weaver clan into her big country kitchen. With another great cook in the family, I started learning Ruby's specialties. Her version of coleslaw is one of them.

Wash and shred a half a gallon of cabbage—about a medium-size head. Dice half a green or mixed red-and-green bell pepper and 2 stalks of celery. Add to the cabbage, along with 1 teaspoon of salt. Mix well with your hand and let stand for 45 minutes.

To make the dressing, mix 1 cup of white vinegar, $\frac{1}{2}$ cup of water, 2 cups of sugar, and 1 teaspoon of celery seed in a stainless-steel saucepan. Heat the dressing just until the sugar dissolves.

After the cabbage has sat for 45 minutes, squeeze the water out of it—there will be quite a bit of it. Pour the dressing over the cabbage and mix well. This coleslaw keeps well and can be frozen by just spooning it into plastic freezer containers. Yields 9 cups.

"MUSKMELON" AND BLACKBERRIES

✦   As you can probably tell by now, we Hoosiers like our sweets. Yet, one of our favorite desserts in the summer was fresh "muskmelons" (the local name for cantaloupes) from the garden. They were difficult to grow and didn't always do well, and when we had a good crop we savored them.

Just cut the melon, peel the skin, seed, and serve very cold. If we had fresh blackberries, they were served on top of the melon with just a dash of sugar. If there were no blackberries, we ate the melon salted.

Family Reunion Picnic

We have these glad reunions
In the Grove or at my home.
We recall the sweet communion
Of loved ones who have gone.
We'll keep alive their memory
Though their faces we can't see.
As we feast on summer's bounty
Spread under the walnut tree.

—Mamaw Tribby

At the end of July, when the tomatoes were ripe and the early corn had matured, we did a lot of visiting. A hundred or more of the Tribby clan got together for our reunions. Grandpa Tribby and his four brothers and four sisters—from Samuel, who was eighteen the year the Civil War broke out, to Grandpa, who was born the year it ended—and all of their children (who hadn't seen each other since the last funeral) came to join in the festivities. Mamaw said the first Tribby reunion was held in 1935 at her house in Old Sylvania, a little village about five miles from our farm, but most were in the grove at the Walnut Grove Church or the yard of the Old Sylvania Church.

Long wooden picnic tables were laden with chicken and dumplings, barbecued ribs, potato salad, baked ham with mashed potatoes and gravy, green beans stewed for hours with a ham bone, ambrosia, wilted lettuce, sliced tomatoes, cucumbers and onions, bread-and-butter pickles, and too many side dishes to mention.

The women all brought their specialties: Mamaw always came with yeast bread and bouquets of black-eyed Susans in mason jars for the tables. Mother made several big trays of raspberry, blackberry, or peach cobblers—she was known far and wide for her exceptional piecrust—to add to the dessert table, which was already loaded down with all kinds of pies, strawberry shortcakes, and devil's food and angel food cakes. Along about four o'clock, one of the ice cream makers would get too hard to crank, so somebody would start dishing up the ice cream.

If there was an important event in the family, or the nation, Mamaw would read the poem she had written about it. One of the girls sang, and my sister Sue played the piano. We didn't have telephones for many years (until I was thirteen), so everybody looked forward to a big get-together to gossip about the old days and brag about their kids!

Come in the evening, or come in the morning,
Come when you're looked for, or come without warning.

—Thomas O. Davis,
"The Welcome"

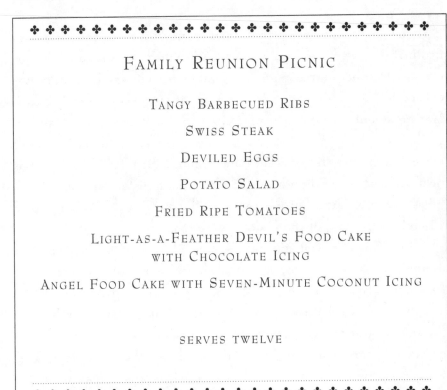

FAMILY REUNION PICNIC

TANGY BARBECUED RIBS

SWISS STEAK

DEVILED EGGS

POTATO SALAD

FRIED RIPE TOMATOES

LIGHT-AS-A-FEATHER DEVIL'S FOOD CAKE
WITH CHOCOLATE ICING

ANGEL FOOD CAKE WITH SEVEN-MINUTE COCONUT ICING

SERVES TWELVE

TANGY BARBECUED RIBS

✦ Make the sauce by sautéing 1 cup of chopped onions and 2 crushed garlic cloves in 2 tablespoons of bacon fat. Add ³/₄ cup of packed dark-brown sugar, 1 cup of ketchup, 3 tablespoons of Worcestershire sauce, 2 tablespoons of prepared mustard, ¹/₂ teaspoon of Tabasco sauce, 1 teaspoon of salt, ¹/₄ cup of white vinegar, and 1¹/₂ cups of water. Stir well, cover, and gently simmer for 10 minutes.

Parboil 6 pounds of pork spareribs for 10 minutes; drain and pat dry. Place on an open grill about 5 inches from the coals. Cook until brown, about 30 minutes. Baste with the sauce, turn, and continue to cook, basting every 5 minutes. Cook until done, about an hour.

SWISS STEAK

✦ Salt and pepper a 4-pound round steak. Pound a cup of flour into it with a meat mallet or a heavy plate.

Heat 3 tablespoons of vegetable oil in a cast-iron skillet. Fast-fry the steak over high heat until browned on both sides, 3 to 5 minutes on each side. Move the steak to a roaster.

Make a gravy by adding 2 tablespoons of flour, 2 teaspoons of soy sauce, and 4 cups of water to the drippings in the skillet. Boil until thickened, stirring frequently. Pour the gravy over the steak.

Cover with a tight lid and bake in a slow oven (300° to 350°) for $1^{1}/_{2}$ to 2 hours, or until the meat is tender. As a variation, you can add a quart of canned tomatoes with their juice and 2 to 3 small onions to the roaster in place of the gravy.

DEVILED EGGS

✦   Would it be a picnic without deviled eggs? Deviled eggs are one of those dishes that most people don't think very much about, but when you slip one of these smooth, savory morsels into your mouth you can't help reaching for a second.

Hard-boil a dozen eggs. Peel them, cut them in half lengthwise, and pop the yolks into a mixing bowl. Mix in mayonnaise or Miracle Whip to make a thick, smooth consistency. Season the mixture with a tablespoon of prepared mustard, just a dash of wine vinegar and Worcestershire sauce, and salt and pepper. Add 10 finely chopped and pitted large black olives. Fill the hard-boiled egg whites with the yolk mixture and sprinkle paprika on them. Chill thoroughly.

POTATO SALAD

✦   I love potato salad when it's sweet and sour and has a wonderful creamy, crunchy texture.

Take about 6 cups of cooked, cubed potatoes (cook them slowly, in the jacket, then you can almost pull the skins off), 4 chopped hard-boiled eggs, 2/3 cup of finely chopped onions (the sweeter the better), 2 teaspoons of salt, 1/2 teaspoon of pepper, 1 chopped green bell pepper, 4 tablespoons of sweet relish, 2 tablespoons of prepared mustard, and 1 cup of mayonnaise or Miracle Whip. Stir together. If it seems drier than you like, add mayonnaise. You can easily double or triple this recipe. We used to make so much for family get-togethers that the only thing that could hold it all was a dishpan. Sprinkle with paprika and chill.

FRIED RIPE TOMATOES

✦   Mamaw Tribby used to say that any housewife who didn't peel her tomatoes was lazy. I always thought that was a little extreme—and now that we know that most of the nutrients are concentrated close to the skin, I feel justified. However, this dish *is* better with peeled tomatoes, because the breading won't stick to the skin.

Wash 5 large tomatoes and cut them into thick, $1/2$-inch slices. Mix 2 slightly beaten eggs in a cup of milk. Bread the tomatoes by dipping each slice in the egg-and-milk mixture, and then dipping it in seasoned bread crumbs—you'll need about 2 cups. Repeat the procedure for two coats of breading. To season the bread crumbs, add $1/4$ teaspoon of each of the following: salt, pepper, dried basil, and garlic powder. Mix well. Fry the tomato slices in butter or vegetable oil over medium heat until golden brown on both sides. Drain on paper towels.

LIGHT-AS-A-FEATHER DEVIL'S FOOD CAKE WITH CHOCOLATE ICING

✦   Sift together three times (count 'em!): 2 cups of flour, 1 teaspoon of baking soda, $1/2$ cup of good cocoa, $1^1/2$ cups of sugar, $1/4$ teaspoon of mace, and $1/2$ teaspoon of salt. Then drop in 2 eggs, 1 teaspoon of vanilla, $1/2$ cup of melted butter, and 1 cup of buttermilk. Beat the ingredients at low speed until they are combined. Beat for another 2 minutes at medium speed until the batter is smooth. Divide the batter between two buttered and floured 9-inch layer-cake pans.

Bake in a preheated 350° oven for 30 to 35 minutes, or until a toothpick or broom straw stuck in the middle of the cake comes out clean. Let the cakes cool in the pans for 10 minutes before inverting onto wire racks. Cool completely before icing.

To make the chocolate icing, melt 3 squares of unsweetened baking chocolate with 3 tablespoons of butter and 7 tablespoons of half-and-half in a small saucepan over a medium heat. Pour a 16-ounce box of confectioners' sugar into a mixing bowl and pour the heated mixture over it. Add a teaspoon of vanilla extract and beat with an electric mixer until the icing is the right consistency for spreading. Add more half-and-half or sugar as needed. Use a quarter of the icing for the filling between the cake layers.

ANGEL FOOD CAKE WITH SEVEN-MINUTE COCONUT ICING

✦   Angel food cake was a light, delicate, and majestic cake saved for special occasions. You *must* use cake flour, because otherwise it just won't turn out right!

Sift cake flour and measure out 1 cup. Add ¼ teaspoon of salt and sift 3 more times. Sift sugar and measure out 1¼ cups.

Beat 1 cup of egg whites (from about a dozen eggs) until foamy. Add a teaspoon of cream of tartar and continue beating until they form soft peaks. Gently fold the sugar mixture into the egg whites, alternating with the sifted flour. Add 1 teaspoon of vanilla extract just before the last of the flour is added.

Pour the batter into an ungreased angel food cake pan (tube). Use a kitchen knife to gently cut through the batter to remove any air bubbles. Bake in a preheated 300° oven for about an hour, or until the top is golden brown and any cracks in the top are dry.

Remove the cake from the oven and immediately turn the pan upside down over a Coke bottle. Let it cool completely—an hour or more—before icing.

Gently slide a spatula or long-bladed knife down the sides of the cake pan to loosen the cake. Turn it out on a cake plate and ice.

To make the icing mix together 2 unbeaten egg whites, 1½ cups of sugar, 1 tablespoon of light corn syrup, and 5 tablespoons of water in the top of a double boiler (off the heat). Beat well with a mixer. Place the top over boiling water and continue beating with the mixer as it cooks for 7 minutes—the icing should peak when its done. Fold

¹/₂ cup of shredded canned coconut into the icing. Ice the sides of the cake and make the icing stand in peaks on top of the cake. Sprinkle ¹/₂ cup of coconut on the top and sides of the cake.

> *I don't want none of your weevily wheat,*
> *I don't want none of your barley,*
> *I want fine flour in half an hour,*
> *To bake a cake for Charley.*

> —folk song

Homemade Ice Cream Makes a Summer Afternoon

I doubt whether the world holds for anyone a more stirring surprise than the first adventure with ice cream.

—Heywood Broun,
Seeing Things at Night

Nothing brings back those summer afternoons of my childhood more than making ice cream. In those days we had never even heard of air conditioning. We were lucky to have a little metal fan rotating in the kitchen, but the only place you could really breathe was in the front yard under the maple tree. All of the big folks sat in a circle in metal lawn chairs, telling stories while the kids lay on the ground on one of Mamaw Tribby's old quilts.

Late in the afternoon, after we had digested our dinner, Mother would say to Daddy, "Wilbur, why don't we have a little ice cream?" And he would go get the big old-fashioned ice cream maker out of the basement with Alan and Jeff tagging along behind him carrying the salt and ice. Sue got the ice-cold metal canister out of the freezer and carefully filled it with the chilled sweet cream and fruit that Mother had mixed up the night before. We all helped pack the old wooden bucket with the salt and ice and fit the canister snugly inside before Daddy sealed the top. Then everybody took their turns at cranking. The kids went first, and as the crank got harder and harder to turn, the men took over. Eventually, the crank couldn't be turned anymore and we had ice cream. I had the best job—licking the wooden paddle.

With all the fancy commercial ice creams that have come out in the last few years, I keep hoping—but none even come close to the taste of old-fashioned homemade ice cream. They just can't produce the intensely rich yet light flavor we got from the old wooden freezer.

✦ ✦

Mamaw Hutchens' Tips for Making Ice Cream

1. Use an old-fashioned hand-crank ice cream maker with a metal canister. My recipes yield 1 gallon; check the capacity of your ice cream maker and adjust the recipe accordingly.

2. Freeze the canister before you pour in the ice cream mixture.

3. Combine the ice cream mixture ahead of time and keep it covered in the refrigerator for at least an hour—if possible, overnight. The more thoroughly chilled the mixture, the faster you'll have ice cream and the smoother it will be.

4. Fine crushed ice makes a smoother-textured ice cream.

5. Fill the canister no more than 3/4 full, since the ice cream expands.

6. Put about 3 inches of ice into the bucket and then some rock salt, then another 3 inches of ice and then salt, and so on. For a gallon of ice cream, you'll need about 20 pounds of crushed ice and 3 cups of rock salt. If you use more salt, the ice cream freezes faster but the texture will not be as smooth.

7. Finished ice cream can be stored in plastic containers in the freezer compartment of your refrigerator. It can be kept for up to a month. Before you serve it, let it soften in the refrigerator for 20 minutes or so.

✦ ✦

HOMEMADE ICE CREAM MAKES A SUMMER AFTERNOON

CAN'T-BE-BEAT VANILLA ICE CREAM

LUSCIOUS STRAWBERRY OR PEACH ICE CREAM

EXTRA-RICH CUSTARD-BASED VANILLA ICE CREAM

CAN'T-BE-BEAT VANILLA ICE CREAM

✦   This is Mamaw Hutchens' junket ice cream. Junket comes in tablet form and thickens the milk. It can be found beside the gelatin products in most grocery stores.

First, dissolve 4 junket tablets in 3 tablespoons of cold water and set aside. Meanwhile, in a large kettle, stir together 1 quart of heavy cream and 1½ quarts of milk. Add 2 cups of sugar and 2 teaspoons of vanilla extract. Mix and set over a low heat until just barely warm. Add a few grains of salt. Keep stirring until warmed through. Remove from the heat and thoroughly stir in the dissolved junket.

Pour the base into the freezer canister and let it sit with the lid on for at least an hour, or until it thickens to a custardy consistency. If possible, let it chill overnight in the refrigerator.

Fill the outside of the freezer with ice and salt as in Mamaw's tip number 6 (on opposite page). You'll need people to crank for 30 to 45 minutes. Makes 1 gallon.

LUSCIOUS STRAWBERRY OR PEACH ICE CREAM

✦   Mamaw Hutchens' junket Can't-Be-Beat Vanilla Ice Cream can be adapted to fruit ice cream if you reduce the milk by about 2 cups and add 2 cups of crushed fresh peaches or strawberries. Reduce the vanilla to 1 teaspoon. Makes 1 gallon.

EXTRA-RICH CUSTARD-BASED VANILLA ICE CREAM

✦   Not everyone likes the distinctive taste of junket ice cream, although our family loved it. Here is a good alternative that is richer, more like what we now call French Vanilla.

Combine 6 eggs and a quart of milk in a saucepan and beat with a wire whisk until well blended. Add 2 cups of sugar and $1/2$ teaspoon of salt. Cook over a low heat, stirring constantly, until the custard thickens to the consistency of a milk shake. Put the saucepan in a basin of cold water and cool to room temperature.

Mix a quart of heavy cream with 5 teaspoons of vanilla extract. Stir the cream and vanilla mixture into the cooled custard. Chill in the refrigerator for at least an hour, or, if possible, overnight.

Pour the custard into a cold freezer canister and start cranking. Makes 1 gallon.

[Happiness] always looks small while you hold it in your hands, but let it go, and you learn at once how big and precious it is.

—Maxim Gorky,
The Zykovs

What's Summer Without Corn?

It seemed as if we could hear the corn growing in the night; under the stars one caught a faint crackling in the dewy, heavy-odoured cornfields where the feathered stalks stood so juicy and green.

—Willa Cather,
My Ántonia

By August, bushel baskets of corn were coming out of the garden every day and we ate so much of it we thought we'd burst! Yet it was always a special treat, and we never tired of it. From the point of view of the cook—me—corn made an ideal meal. Picking and shucking three or four ears for each of the six of us was the hardest part, but then all I had to do was let it boil. The corn pot was a big old black thing that had been my Grandmother Flo's. In the height of the season, corn became the main dish set in the center of the table on a china meat platter with its golden kernels steaming and sparkling. All I added was some sliced tomatoes and cucumbers and onions on the side and homemade bread and jelly.

Eating corn was considered a sport in our family. The sight and sound of the six of us making so much noise always made me laugh. There we were, chomping away, our noisy rhythm going up a row and back, now and then adding another stripped cob to the growing pile. Of course, the real reason we ate so much was because it tasted so good. Whether it was Golden Bantam, Daddy's favorite, or Country Gentleman, we always had yellow corn. As Daddy reminded us every summer, "The yellow is what makes it nutritious." If we had a lot of rain, even field corn, like Reid's Yellow Dent, was quite delicate just after it tasseled.

From the left, Alan, Jeff, me, and Sue playing on a July day.

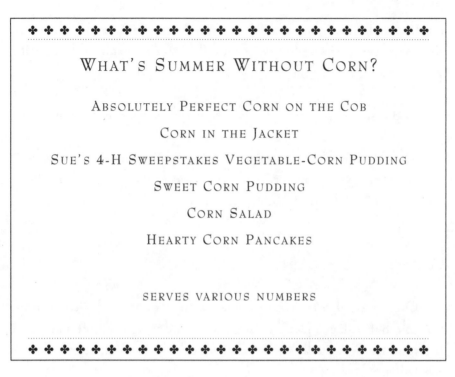

✦ ✦

WHAT'S SUMMER WITHOUT CORN?

ABSOLUTELY PERFECT CORN ON THE COB

CORN IN THE JACKET

SUE'S 4-H SWEEPSTAKES VEGETABLE-CORN PUDDING

SWEET CORN PUDDING

CORN SALAD

HEARTY CORN PANCAKES

SERVES VARIOUS NUMBERS

✦ ✦

ABSOLUTELY PERFECT CORN ON THE COB

✦ Some people say you should boil corn in milk. In my opinion that is something no country person would ever do, because it is such an unbelievable waste. People who eat corn on the cob two times a day from mid-July through August would have used more milk than their old cow could give. The liquid is just a vehicle to cook the corn in—the flavor is exclusively its own. The most important thing you can do to enhance the flavor of corn on the cob is to cook it *immediately* after it is picked.

Bring a very large pot of water to a boil. While the water is boiling, pick and shuck the corn. Remove any silk, bad spots, and the ends of the cobs. When the water boils, stack the cobs one on top of the other, making sure the water completely covers the corn. Let boil for 5 minutes. If it's late in the season and the ears are beginning to get a little tough, cook the corn for an extra 3 or 4 minutes. Remove with tongs and serve piping hot with lots of butter and salt, although it's great without a thing on it.

A pug nose comes in mighty handy during the roasting ear season.

—Abe Martin, Brown County, Indiana, "philosopher" and much-loved cartoon character in *The Indianapolis News,* written in the early 1900s by Kim Hubbard

CORN IN THE JACKET

✦   Oven-roasted corn is a nice change from everyday boiled corn on the cob, but it does mean heating the oven during the hottest days of the summer. We usually tried to bake a cake at the same time that we roasted corn.

Pull the husks back on each ear but leave attached to the stalk end; remove the silk. For about a dozen ears, melt 1 cup of butter and add a teaspoon of salt to it. Use a pastry brush to generously spread the butter on the raw corn. You can add a spice like garlic to the butter if you want.

Pull the husks back up and tie them at the top of each ear with a piece of string. Bake in a preheated 375° oven for 45–50 minutes for average-sized ears. Serve hot.

SUE'S 4-H SWEEPSTAKES VEGETABLE-CORN PUDDING

✦   When the Greene County Fair rolled around in August, one thing we could count on was my sister Sue winning the 4-H Club's purple ribbon for sewing. One year Mother's Aunt Velma, who always wore a freshly ironed apron and her braided hair high on top of her head, gave Sue the recipe for this creamy, rich casserole, and then she also took the sweepstakes in cooking! After that, it became Sue's specialty.

Mix together a tablespoon of flour, $1/4$ teaspoon of coarse-ground pepper, 1 well-beaten egg, half a diced green bell pepper, one 16-ounce can of creamed corn, $1/2$ teaspoon of salt, a tablespoon of sugar, and a dash of paprika. Pour into a buttered 9-inch square baking dish. Bake in a 375° oven until firm and well browned on top, about 45 minutes. Serves six.

As a variation I like to substitute fresh or frozen corn for canned creamed corn—the texture is less like a pudding. Use 2 cups of fresh corn, cut from the cobs, or loosened frozen corn. Add 2 cups of milk, 2 tablespoons of melted butter, and an extra egg. Serves six.

SWEET CORN PUDDING

✦ Cut 4 cups of corn off of the cobs, getting as much milk from the cobs as you can. Put into the top of a double boiler and add $3^1/4$ cups of half-and-half, 3 well-beaten eggs, $1/2$ cup of butter, and $1/2$ cup of sugar. Set over boiling water and cook until the corn mixture begins to thicken to the consistency of a milk shake, about 10 minutes.

Turn out into a large buttered baking dish. Bake in a preheated 375° oven for about 1 hour, or until browned and firm. Makes 18 to 20 servings.

CORN SALAD

✦ Cut the corn off of 6 ears of fresh sweet corn. Dice 3 green bell peppers, 5 or 6 stalks of celery, and a small onion or 5 or 6 scallions. Combine all of the vegetables in a stainless-steel saucepan and add $1/2$ cup of apple cider vinegar, $1/2$ cup of water, $1/2$ cup of sugar, $1/2$ teaspoon of salt, $1/2$ teaspoon of dry mustard, and a teaspoon of celery seeds. Bring to a boil. Reduce the heat to low and simmer for 5 to 8 minutes, or until the corn is cooked but still very firm and crunchy. Refrigerate in a covered dish until chilled thoroughly. Serves six.

HEARTY CORN PANCAKES

✦   If you make these for breakfast, you can have corn for three meals a day.

On a sheet of waxed paper, sift together 1¼ cups of flour, a teaspoon of baking powder, and ½ teaspoon of salt. In a mixing bowl, stir together 2 beaten eggs, 1 cup of milk, and 2 tablespoons of vegetable oil. Add the dry ingredients and stir together. Stir in 2 cups of corn cut from the cobs. Frozen corn, thawed and drained, can be used also. If the batter is too thick to spread, add a little more milk.

Ladle the batter onto a hot, greased griddle and cook until the edges brown and bubbles form on the top. Flip and cook on the other side. Serve at once, with maple syrup and butter. Makes enough pancakes to serve six.

✦ ✦

Now, one year we was kind of late puttin' in our crops. Everybody else had corn a foot high when papa said, "Well, chillun, Ah reckon we better plant some corn." So Ah was droppin' and my brother was hillin' up behind me. We had done planted 'bout a dozen rows when Ah looked back and seen de corn comin' up. Ah didn't want it to grow too fast 'cause it would make all fodder and no roastin' ears so Ah hollered to my brother to sit down on some of it to stunt de growth. So he did, and de next day he dropped me back a note—says: "passed thru Heben yesterday at twelve o'clock sellin' roastin' ears to de angels."

—Zora Neale Hurston, *Mules and Men*

✦ ✦

There is no dignity in the bean. Corn, with no affectation of superiority, is however, the child of song.

—Charles Dudley Warner,
My Summer in a Garden

AUTUMN

Making Cider and Filling Silos

O, it sets my hart a-clickin' like the
    tickin' of a clock,
When the frost is on the punkin and the
    fodder's in the shock!

—James Whitcomb Riley,
    "When the Frost Is on the Punkin"

Apple Pickin' Time

Among the weeds and scattered stones,
Lie the Old Home's broken bones.
But each autumn straight and tall
Apple trees grow against the wall.
Red and gold each apple sparkles,
Bright against old stone markers.
She who planted them has passed,
Not dreaming of their colors—now massed
Against the ruin of a house
Inhabited by rat and mouse.
Yet, the planting of her hands
Is a monument that stands.

—Mamaw Tribby

Mother was twelve when Mamaw and Grandpa Tribby lost the family homestead at Walnut Valley during the Depression. A distant relative turned the lovely old farm into a tobacco barn with a commercial apple orchard and a sorghum mill. Every apple season Mother loaded us into the Ford to go to the orchard in Walnut Valley. We always walked back up to the house where Mother was born, and every year it looked more and more run-down and forlorn. Finally, we couldn't even go inside for fear the floorboards would break.

I think we loved that old orchard almost as much as she did. Every October the Winesap, Rome Beauty, and Jonathan trees drooped from the weight of fruit that grew in every shade of red from blush to maroon. Mother and Sue picked from the branches they could reach while I gathered the apples on the ground and Alan and Jeff climbed the trees. When we paid for the apples we always bought several gallons of sweet cider and big jars of the black sorghum that Daddy loved to mix with butter and spread on homemade bread for a winter snack.

When we were at the orchard, we always got enough apples for Mother to make fifty to sixty pints of her special apple butter, which was very dark, sweet, and rich. In the winter we had it almost every day for breakfast with toast. Making apple butter is quite a production. She always called it her "easy twenty-minute" apple butter recipe. Right! After you peel about three hundred apples, core them, quarter them, cook them, and rub them through a colander, *then* it takes only twenty minutes.

One day after school I heard heaving sobs coming from the kitchen. When I got there I saw Mother sitting on the floor with her back against the cabinet, surrounded by apples, apple peels, and jars. She was wiping her eyes with the tail of her apron and trying to stop crying. By then my brothers were behind me and we were all terrified. She just kept saying, "Salt, salt, salt . . ." For the longest time we couldn't figure out what she was trying to tell us. Salt and sugar were both stored in bulk in big pullout wooden bins next to each other in our kitchen, and she had used salt instead of sugar in about fifty pints of apple butter. That batch wasn't so sweet!

*Grandpa Tribby picking apples in the orchard
at Walnut Valley.*

*Remember Johnny Appleseed,
All ye who love the apple;
He served his kind by word and deed,
In God's grand greenwood chapel.*

—William Henry Venable,
"Johnny Appleseed"

October, 1930

I went back to Walnut Valley, our old home place, today--
about a year after we had left it. The walls of the old house that
used to ring with children's laughter are as silent as the grave. The
old house just sits and dreams the years and days away. The
orchard is overgrown with weeds and fruit is rolling under the
trees. My dear friend, the apple tree by the spring, is dressed in red
and gold to welcome me home.

Today I climbed the old stone steps now covered with its dead
leaves. Inside the house, was there a light footstep? Someone
seemed to whisper to me. It was only the autumn wind, and the
child I thought I heard could come back no more. My heart was
flooded with a thousand memories-- of this room where I used to sit
in the winter with my quilt pieces, Dad with his newspaper and
the children, especially my beloved Troy, playing on the floor; of
the garden where they caught ladybugs while we hoed at the end
of a summer's day.

Bessie Tribby

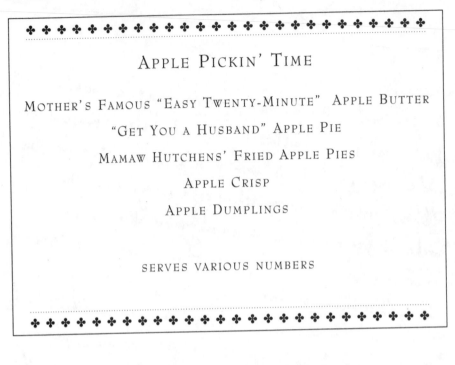

❋ ❋

APPLE PICKIN' TIME

MOTHER'S FAMOUS "EASY TWENTY-MINUTE" APPLE BUTTER

"GET YOU A HUSBAND" APPLE PIE

MAMAW HUTCHENS' FRIED APPLE PIES

APPLE CRISP

APPLE DUMPLINGS

SERVES VARIOUS NUMBERS

❋ ❋

MOTHER'S FAMOUS "EASY TWENTY-MINUTE" APPLE BUTTER

❖ Peel and slice about 4½ pounds of apples—enough to cook down to 3 pints of pulp. To make the pulp, combine the apples with a ¼ cup of apple cider and ¼ cup of water in a saucepan. Cook over medium heat until soft, about 10 minutes.

Rub the cooked apples along with all of the cooking liquid through a colander into a kettle. Add 3 cups of sugar, 3 tablespoons of redhots (cinnamon imperials), and ¼ cup of cider vinegar. Boil the apples, stirring frequently, for 20 minutes, or until thick. Serve with homemade bread. This will keep in the refrigerator for 2 weeks if sealed tightly. Makes 3 pints.

To put away for the winter, spoon boiling apple butter into sterile pint jars, leaving half an inch of head space. Wipe the rim well. Seal with self-sealing, sterile lids, following the manufacturer's instructions. Process, using the boiling-water method, for 10 minutes.

Consult with the United States Department of Agriculture guidelines for exact instructions for your area.

"Get You a Husband" Apple Pie

✦ I've yet to meet a man who isn't thrilled when his sweetheart makes him an apple pie—just slightly sweet, laced with a hint of cinnamon in a flaky two-crust pastry. If you're the sweetheart, you want the pie to be nice and high, with firm, large slices that retain their shape and a well-browned top with juice bubbling out of its slits. As Mother used to tell me, such a pie might not get you a husband, but then again, it might.

The two most common mistakes people make with apple pie are using too much sugar and overwhelming the subtle flavor of the apples with spices. A dash of lemon helps to eliminate the syrupy taste that ruins a pie. As much as I like sweet spices, nutmeg, clove, and allspice have no place in an apple pie. Cinnamon is enough. Taste your filling as you are making it—apples vary in sweetness. The apples that make the best pies are MacIntosh, Cortland, Rome Beauty, Arkansas, and Tolman Sweet. Skinny pies always look sad to me, so I pour the apples into the crust and use my hands to gently pile up as much fruit as I can.

Peel and core 7 medium apples, each cut into eighths. Add 1 cup of sugar, 3 rounded tablespoons of flour, 1 teaspoon of cinnamon, and 2 teaspoons of lemon juice. Toss to mix well.

Line the bottom of a deep-dish 9-inch pie pan with an unbaked piecrust (see page 34).

Pour the apples into the crust and use your hands to pile the fruit as high as you can. Dot the top with 1 or 2 tablespoons of butter. Cover with a top crust, flute the edges, make 2 slits shaped like half-moons, and generously prick the top crust with a knife.

Bake in a preheated 450° oven for 1 hour, or until browned on top. I put aluminum foil around the edges during the first 40 minutes of baking so the fluted edge doesn't get too brown. An old beat-up baking sheet can be used under the pie to catch any drips as it bakes. Makes 1 pie.

MAMAW HUTCHENS' FRIED APPLE PIES

◆ Mamaw Hutchens was raised in Alabama, so she cooked a lot of Southern favorites, like this one. These luscious little gems were a special treat—especially when we would find them in our lunch boxes!

In a saucepan, melt 1/4 cup of butter. Add about 4 cups of thinly sliced apples, 1/2 cup of sugar (taste after it cooks a while and add more if necessary), a teaspoon of mixed cinnamon, nutmeg, and allspice, and a teaspoon of lemon juice. Cook, stirring frequently, over a medium heat for 5 minutes. When the apples begin to form juice, turn the heat to low. Dissolve a tablespoon of cornstarch in 1/4 cup of cold water and add to the apples. Stir constantly until the apples are quite soft and the juice is thick and smooth, 10 to 15 minutes. Let cool to room temperature before using.

Make the piecrust recipe from page 34, and divide the dough in half. Roll out each piece to the same thickness. With a sharp paring knife, cut the dough into circles about 6 inches wide. After you cut as many pieces as you can from the dough (at least 3), knead the leftovers together and roll out again to make another circle.

Place about 2 tablespoonfuls of the apple filling in the center of the dough and fold it over. (Use as much filling as you can and still fold the dough over.) Seal the edges of each pie securely by moistening them lightly and pressing them together with the prongs of a fork.

Heat 1/2 cup of oil or melted shortening in a cast-iron skillet until it is hot. Carefully place some of the pies in the hot fat and fry over low heat until they are browned on each side, about 15 to 20 minutes per side. Makes about 8 fried pies.

APPLE CRISP

✦   Butter a 9-inch square baking dish. Peel, core, and slice enough apples to measure 4 cups. Pour the apples into the baking dish and add ³/₄ cup of boiling water.

In a mixing bowl, cream together ¹/₃ cup of butter with ³/₄ cup of sugar. Mix in ¹/₂ cup of flour, 1¹/₂ teaspoons of cinnamon, 1 teaspoon of vanilla, and ¹/₂ teaspoon of lemon extract; stir until the mixture is crumbly. Scatter this mixture evenly over the apples.

Bake in a preheated 400° oven for 45 minutes, or until browned on top. Serve with sweetened whipped cream. Makes 9 servings.

APPLE DUMPLINGS

✦   Peel, core, and thinly slice 4 apples. In a bowl, combine the apples, ¹/₂ cup of sugar, and ³/₄ teaspoon of cinnamon; toss well and set aside, tossing from time to time.

To make a dough, combine 2 cups of flour and ³/₄ teaspoon of salt. Cut in ¹/₂ cup of butter with a pastry blender. Add 5–7 tablespoons of ice water or enough to make a dough that can be gathered into a ball. Don't handle the dough more than necessary or it will become tough. Divide the dough in half.

On a floured board, roll out each piece of dough into a 10-inch square. Cut each piece of dough into four 5-inch squares. Spoon about 2 tablespoons of the apple mixture in the middle of each square. Add a small dab of butter on top of the apples. Take the four corners of each square and bring them together on top of the apple mixture; pinch them so they stick together into an attractive peak. Pinch each of the four side seams so the juices won't leak out. (Moisten your fingers with cold water before you pinch the seams.) Arrange the dumplings, so they don't touch on a large, greased baking sheet. Bake in a preheated 375° oven for 30 minutes, or until browned. Serve hot, with vanilla ice cream. If desired, glaze the dumplings with an egg wash (1 beaten egg mixed with a little cold water) just before you bake them. Makes 8 servings.

Uncle John is sick a-bed,
What shall we send him?
A piece of pie, a piece of cake,
A piece of apple dumpling.

—folk song

Sweet Potato Pie

He could fiddle all the bugs off a sweet potato vine.

—Stephen Vincent Benét,
"The Mountain Whippoorwill"

All the Tribby women were deeply spiritual. It came naturally with giving birth, growing a garden, taking care of everybody and everything around you, and then having to give it all up at some point. With the men, appreciation of God seemed to come later in life and called for more of a public declaration. The men usually ended up in the pulpit, like my mother's cousin, Chaine.

Chaine was an exceptionally good-looking man with dark wavy hair and a deep and melodious voice. You couldn't have an ordinary conversation with Chaine—about how the corn was doing or whether we'd get rain—without religion working its way in. And pretty soon he would be testifying. Daddy, who was genuinely tolerant of other people, used to say, "Oh, Chaine gets a little radical once in a while, but that's just his way. "

Chaine farmed with his dad, Orville—Mamaw Tribby's brother—all week, but every Sunday he put on a suit and preached the gospel at the Old Sylvania Methodist Church, where all the Tribbys and everybody else in Old Sylvania went to hear him.

If Chaine had ever tried, I'm sure he could have rid the sweet potato vine of bugs as well.

SWEET POTATO PIE

✦ Mash 2 cups of hot, cooked sweet potatoes and add 1 cup of sugar, 1¼ teaspoons of cinnamon, ¼ cup of heavy cream, ¼ cup of melted butter, and ½ teaspoon of salt. Stir well. Beat 2 egg yolks and add ½ cup of heavy cream; fold into the sweet potato mixture. Beat the 2 egg whites until stiff. Fold them into the pie filling.

Pour into an unbaked piecrust (see page 34). Don't add a top crust. Bake in a preheated oven at 450° for about 10 minutes. Reduce the heat to 400° and leave it in for another 30 minutes, or until the pie is firm and the crust is browned. Makes 1 pie.

Feeding the Silo Fillers

Up from the meadows rich with corn,
Clear in the cool September morn.

—John Greenleaf Whittier,
"Barbara Frietchie"

*S*ilo-filling time! Silos were tall towers set near the barn and dwarfed everything else on the horizon. By late November, if there'd been enough rain, they were filled to the brim with silage—a pungent and nutritious feed for the cattle. Silage was made when Daddy and Grandpa went back over the cornfields and chopped up the stalks. As farmers, we were always at the mercy of the weather, but we rarely felt it more than when we were trying to beat the first serious frost. In March of some years you could see acres of frozen cornstalks still standing in the fields of a poor farmer who didn't make it in time.

With us children in school, the only way to get the work done was if the neighbors pitched in to help. Daddy and Grandpa exchanged labor with our closest neighbors, Mr. Weaver and Mr. Langoff, and sometimes extra hands were hired. Wonderful neighbor ladies, like Eula Price, Louise Dye, and Marjorie Frye, always helped Mother and Mamaw Hutchens cook for our silo fillers. Many an evening before, Mother and I made three or four pumpkin pies and a squash cake after the supper dishes were cleared away.

Every year my brothers and I felt that we missed all the excitement by being in school. As hard as we tried, Mother wouldn't even consider letting us play hooky. So the minute we got home from school, we raced straight to the barnyard, the center of action. As soon as we reached the gate, clouds of cornstalk bits with the yeasty, unforgettable smell of silage made it almost impossible to breathe. The deafening noise of wagons moving, men yelling, and the conveyor belt carrying the silage up the outside of the silo to dump it over the top let us know that we weren't too late.

From the left, Daddy, Grandpa Hutchens, Alan, and Jeff
bringing in the early harvest.

Iron rungs traced the side of the silo like a big ladder. Daddy was constantly climbing up the rungs to see how it was packing and then down again to see what was happening on the ground. After a silo was full, he would walk around on the top and stomp it down. No one ever said a word. We all held our breath at that moment—for fear of a disaster, and in awe of the strange grace he had as he was suspended in the middle of the blue October sky.

> *He planted his corn in the month of June*
> *And in July it was knee high;*
> *First of September came a big frost*
> *And all of this young man's corn was lost.*

—folk song, "Young Man Wouldn't Hoe Corn"

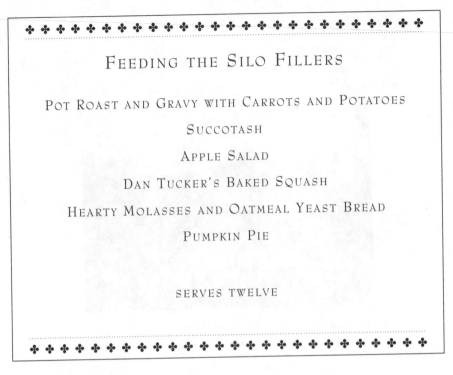

FEEDING THE SILO FILLERS

POT ROAST AND GRAVY WITH CARROTS AND POTATOES

SUCCOTASH

APPLE SALAD

DAN TUCKER'S BAKED SQUASH

HEARTY MOLASSES AND OATMEAL YEAST BREAD

PUMPKIN PIE

SERVES TWELVE

POT ROAST AND GRAVY WITH CARROTS AND POTATOES

✦ Wash a 5-pound rump roast and rub it with each of the following: 1 tablespoon of salt, 1 tablespoon of pepper, and 2 teaspoons of garlic powder. Barely cover the bottom of a Dutch oven with vegetable oil and heat until hot. Put the roast in and brown it on all sides; it needs to get quite brown to keep the juices inside as it stews. Add enough water to the pot to reach about 1/4 to 1/3 of the way up the sides of the roast, but don't pour the water over the meat: pour it in around the sides. Add 3 to 4 whole small onions on each side of the roast. Cover the pot and simmer over a very low heat for about 3 hours, or until the meat is tender.

Peel and quarter 10 carrots, cut lengthwise, and 6 large potatoes. Place them around the roast and continue simmering until the vegetables are tender, about 30 minutes. Test the vegetables with a fork.

When done, remove the roast and place it on a large serving platter. Alternate the potatoes and carrots around the edge of the roast on the serving platter.

To make gravy, bring the pan drippings to a boil over high heat. Add 5 to 6 rounded tablespoons of flour and cook briefly, stirring all the time, until the lumps are out and the flour is cooked. Season with salt and pepper. Serve the gravy hot, in a gravy boat.

SUCCOTASH

✦ Cook 2 pounds of lima beans until they are tender. Drain.

While the limas are cooking, cut the kernels off 8 ears of corn and scrape the milk from the cobs. Sauté a sliced large onion in 3 tablespoons of bacon fat. Add the corn and 1 cup of half-and-half and cook for 10 minutes, or until the corn is tender.

Stir in the limas and cook briefly until heated through. Season with salt and pepper.

APPLE SALAD

✦ Red and yellow apples make a pretty combination in this dish.

Core and dice 8 large unpeeled apples. Sprinkle with $1/2$ cup of sugar and $1/4$ cup of lemon juice. Add 2 cups of raisins, 2 cups of black walnut pieces, and 2 cups of chopped celery. Mix with $1 1/2$ cups of mayonnaise or Miracle Whip—or just enough to hold it together. Served well chilled.

DAN TUCKER'S BAKED SQUASH

✦ Squash for supper was a cue for Daddy to sing "Old Dan Tucker." While growing up, I thought Dan Tucker was actually a neighbor of ours.

Wash and cut 6 acorn squashes in half and scoop out the seeds. Lightly brush the squash inside and out with melted butter. Set the squashes, cut side down, on a greased baking sheet. Bake in a preheated 375° oven for 30 minutes.

Turn the squash halves over and put a dab of butter in each squash. Add a couple of drops of cooking sherry and $1/2$ teaspoon of brown sugar to each. Bake for another 20 minutes, or until browned and the pulp is soft. Serve the squash halves hot.

Old Dan Tucker was a fine old man,
He washed his face with a frying pan,
He combed his hair with a wagon wheel
And died with a toothache in his heel.
Git out the way for old Dan Tucker!
He's too late to git his supper.
Supper's over and dishes washed,
Nothing left but a piece of squash!

—Daniel Decatur Emmett,
"Old Dan Tucker"

HEARTY MOLASSES AND OATMEAL YEAST BREAD

✦ When we made this bread for silo fillers, we always used unbleached white flour because dark flours were considered too heavy for company. If you prefer a dense loaf, just substitute up to 50 percent whole wheat flour as you are making it. You can also knead in a cup of raisins or chopped dates if you like.

In a big ceramic bowl, combine 1 cup of unbleached flour, 2 cups of uncooked old-fashioned oats, 1 teaspoon of salt, and 2 packages of active dry yeast.

Heat 1 cup of milk, $1/2$ cup of water, $3/4$ cup of molasses, and $1/2$ cup of butter in a saucepan until just warm; the butter won't completely melt. Add to the flour and oats and beat very well with an electric mixer. Add 2 eggs at room temperature and another cup of unbleached flour and mix on high for a couple of minutes, or until the eggs and flour are completely integrated into the batter. Continue adding flour, mixing it in with your hands until the dough pulls away from the sides of the bowl—you'll need about 6 cups of flour.

Turn the dough out onto a floured board and knead until it is elastic and "puffy," about 300 turns, or about 10 minutes.

Grease a big bowl and put the dough in it. Turn the dough over so the greased side is up. Cover the dough and let it rise in a warm spot until it doubles in bulk, about 1 hour.

Punch down the dough and let it rise again until doubled, 30 to 45 minutes.

Knead the dough slightly and divide into 2 equal pieces. Grease 2 loaf pans. Make the dough into loaves by rolling each piece into a log about 8 inches long with your hands. Place it, seam side down, in the loaf pan. Lightly flatten out the top and shape the loaves in the pan. Cover with a damp tea towel and let rise until doubled again, about 1 hour.

Brush the top of each loaf with an egg wash (a beaten egg mixed with a little cold water). Bake in a preheated 400° oven for about 30 minutes, or until browned and the loaf sounds hollow when tapped. Makes 2 loaves.

PUMPKIN PIE

✦   For each pie, mix 2 cups of cooked pumpkin with 1 cup of sugar, 1/4 cup of brown sugar, 2 teaspoons of cinnamon, 1/2 teaspoon of nutmeg, a dash of ground cloves, and 1/2 teaspoon of salt. Fold in 3 beaten eggs and a cup of half-and-half.

Pour into an unbaked 9-inch piecrust (see page 34).

Bake in a preheated 400° oven for about 45 minutes, or until the crust is browned and a paring knife inserted a couple of inches from the edge of the pie comes out clean.

Plain Country Cookin'

Wilful waste brings woeful want
And you may live to say,
How I wish I had that crust
That once I threw away.

—Thomas Fuller, "Gnomologia"

No one had very much money in eastern Greene County—at least no one that we knew. And none of the farmers knew how much money they would actually make on their corn or cattle until the day they went to market. Self-reliance was taken for granted. Almost everybody grew their own food, made their own clothes, fixed their own machinery, and built their own houses. In their own ways, Mamaw Tribby and Daddy taught us that happiness came from lots of love and having just enough money to get by. In the winter, when Mamaw Tribby would get a mailbox full of nursery catalogues filled with exotic new flowers that she couldn't afford, she would sit down and look through all the pictures, and then cut out the special ones for her scrapbooks. After a while she would look up and say, "Money might buy a flower, but it takes love to make it bloom."

Expensive ingredients were a rare luxury in Mamaw Tribby's kitchen, but she could rustle up a delicious and satisfying meal from almost nothing—a head of cabbage, a handful of green tomatoes, or maybe a few apples. Daddy always said that Mamaw Tribby could do more with less than anyone he knew. These simple but appetizing dishes were her daily standbys.

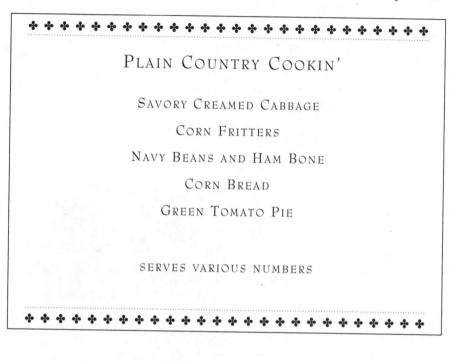

✦ ✦

PLAIN COUNTRY COOKIN'

SAVORY CREAMED CABBAGE

CORN FRITTERS

NAVY BEANS AND HAM BONE

CORN BREAD

GREEN TOMATO PIE

SERVES VARIOUS NUMBERS

✦ ✦

SAVORY CREAMED CABBAGE

✦ Discard the tough outer leaves from a head of cabbage; cut the head into quarters and cut out the core. Cut each quarter in half lengthwise.

Fry 4 to 5 slices of bacon in a cast-iron skillet until it is crisp. Remove the bacon, drain on paper towels, and set aside. Dump the cabbage in the skillet and quickly fry over a high heat, 3 to 5 minutes, until slightly browned. Turn down the heat to low and pour about 1 cup of chicken broth or water over the cabbage, just enough to steam it. Cover and simmer for 10 to 15 minutes. Add a cup of heavy cream and let the cabbage cook over low heat until it is tender but still firm, another 5 to 10 minutes. Do not boil.

Season with salt, coarse-ground pepper, and the bacon crumbled on top. Try it with corn fritters. Serves six.

Old Mister Rabbit,
You've got a mighty habit
Of jumping in the garden
And eating all my cabbage.

—folk song

CORN FRITTERS

✦   In a mixing bowl, beat an egg with 1 cup of milk. Sift together 3 tablespoons of sugar, 1½ cups of flour, 1 tablespoon of baking powder, and ½ teaspoon of salt on a sheet of waxed paper. Stir the dry ingredients into the egg and milk. Add 1 cup of cooked, drained, whole-kernel corn (fresh, frozen, or canned) and 3 tablespoons of melted butter and stir into the batter. The mixture should be the consistency of a cake batter; if it's too thin, gradually add more flour.

Ladle a little less than ¼ cup of the batter onto a buttered hot griddle and flatten out to the desired thickness. We liked them thicker than pancakes—about ½ inch. Brown on both sides and serve immediately. Makes 14 to 16 fritters.

Navy Beans and Ham Bone

✦   We had beans about once a week, and they were always taken for granted. Mother called them Depression food. They stretched the budget and could be left on the stove to cook by themselves when she was busy and the rest of us were in school. On washdays in the fall and winter months, Daddy used to ask for the "washday blue plate special," navy beans and corn bread. We liked navy beans, but also ate a lot of great northern and pinto beans. Mother thought it was really funny that when I became a vegetarian for a while in college I was eating beans every day and *bragging* about it!

    If you don't have a ham bone, bacon can be used in its place—drop in 3 or 4 strips of bacon cut into 3-inch pieces just as the beans are beginning to boil.

    Check 2½ cups of dried beans and throw out anything that doesn't look like it should be there. Wash them and soak overnight in cold water.

    Rinse well and pour the beans into a large pot. Add 2 quarts of water, a smoked ham bone with some meat left on it, 3 or 4 very small whole onions, and 5 peppercorns. Bring to a boil. Reduce the heat to the lowest setting and simmer until the beans are tender, 3 to 4 hours. Check periodically to see if they need water and add it, a cup at a time, if they are getting dry.

    Season the beans with salt and pepper. Remove the ham bone. Pick off any meat that remains on the bone and discard the bone. If you want to thicken the soup, mash up ¼ cup of beans in a separate bowl and add a teaspoon of flour and enough soup liquid to make a paste. Stir it into the beans and cook, stirring, until thickened. Serve over corn bread. Makes 10 servings.

CORN BREAD

✦   Preheat the oven to 425°. Place 2 tablespoons of bacon fat in the middle of a 9-inch or 10-inch cast-iron skillet and put it in the oven until the grease melts.

Sift the following dry ingredients together in a mixing bowl: 1 cup of yellow cornmeal, 1 cup of flour, 2 tablespoons of sugar, 1 tablespoon of baking powder, and 1 teaspoon of salt. Add 1¼ cups of milk and 1 slightly beaten egg. Stir just until mixed. Pour the hot bacon fat into the batter and stir. Pour the batter into the skillet.

Bake until the top is a crusty brown, about 20 minutes. Serve hot. Makes 8 pie-shaped wedges.

If thee needs anything and cannot find it, just come to me and I'll tell thee how to get along without it.

—Etta Macy, quoted by James Alexander Thom in
  "Indiana's Self-Reliant Uplanders," *National Geographic*

GREEN TOMATO PIE

✦   Wash and slice 6 or 7 green tomatoes into a large skillet. Mix in 3 tablespoons of lemon juice, 2 teaspoons of grated lemon rind, 1 cup of sugar, ½ teaspoon of cinnamon, and ¼ teaspoon of salt. Cook over a low heat until the tomatoes are tender, about 15 minutes.

Dissolve 4 tablespoons of cornstarch in ¼ cup of cold water. Add to the tomatoes and cook over a medium heat, stirring constantly, until the liquid is clear, about 5 minutes. Taste the filling and add sugar, lemon, or cinnamon as needed. Stir in 1 tablespoon of butter. Set aside to cool enough so that the filling won't burn your fingers if you happen to touch it as you prepare the crust.

Pour the filling into an unbaked piecrust (see page 34) and top with a solid crust. Flute the edges, cut 2 slits, and use a knife to prick the top.

Bake in a preheated 425° oven for 45 minutes, or until the top is browned. Makes 1 pie.

WINTER

Keeping Warm with Stews and Soups

In the bleak midwinter
Frosty wind made moan,
Earth stood hard as iron,
Water like a stone;
Snow had fallen, snow on snow,
Snow on snow,
In the bleak midwinter,
Long ago.

—Christina Rossetti,
    "A Christmas Carol"

Winter Breakfast on the Farm

Over the woodlands brown and bare,
Over the harvest-fields forsaken,
Silent, and soft, and slow
Descends the snow.

—Henry Wadsworth Longfellow,
"Snow-flakes"

The garden in winter.

After rushing to get the crops in and clear the garden before the frost, the stillness of the first serious snowfall was a welcome relief. In mid-December a damp coldness that penetrated even my young bones settled in for the duration of the winter. From Thanksgiving until March several blizzards with drifts as high as a man's head wrapped the farm in a frosty white quilt. The fences and sheds were snow-covered lumps in a vast wintery sea.

In the frigid pre-dawn, Mother would be in the kitchen, her head bent over the counter as she cut biscuit dough and made coffee. We children grabbed our clothes and ran to the living room to dress for school in front of the fireplace—the only warm spot in the house at 6:00 A.M. We could hear Daddy  shaking the snow off his boots as he came in from the early chores. His face was red as he sat down to hot plates of ham and eggs, biscuits and gravy, pancakes, and fried potatoes. We took our places at the table and devoured enough good food to sustain us through the cold morning. Since we weren't allowed to drink coffee yet, Mother made us hot tea from the bark of the sassafras tree. Even without caffeine, its sweet pungent aroma finally woke us. After breakfast, I stood at the kitchen window, washing dishes as the orange sun came up over the garden.

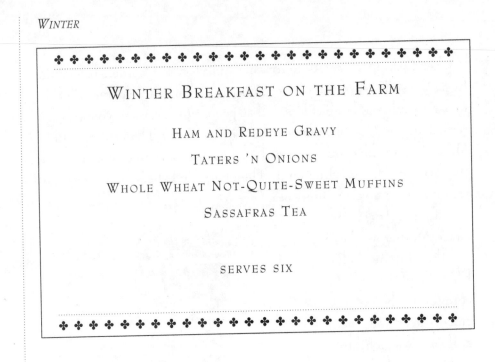

WINTER BREAKFAST ON THE FARM

HAM AND REDEYE GRAVY

TATERS 'N ONIONS

WHOLE WHEAT NOT-QUITE-SWEET MUFFINS

SASSAFRAS TEA

SERVES SIX

HAM AND REDEYE GRAVY

✦ Heat a large cast-iron skillet until it is very hot. Cut off the rind but not the fat of $2\frac{1}{2}$ to 3 pounds of thick-sliced, cooked, country ham. Fry the ham slowly, cooking it thoroughly on one side at a time, and try to turn it just once. (Cutting slits in the ham will help keep it from curling on the edges.) The fat should sizzle and brown as it cooks. When it's nice and brown, take the ham out of the skillet and keep it warm.

To make the gravy, add to the skillet any extra ham fat you have left over, $\frac{1}{4}$ cup of water, 1 cup of strong coffee, and a tablespoon of dark-brown sugar or molasses. Bring to a boil over medium heat. While you stir, scrape the bottom of the skillet to loosen the stuck ham. Reduce the heat to low and simmer for about 5 minutes, or until the gravy thickens a little. Take out the ham fat and then pour the gravy over the ham.

TATERS 'N ONIONS

◆   Taters 'n onions were a staple in our house at any meal, any time of the year.

Peel and slice 8 medium potatoes. Heat a cast-iron skillet with 1/3 cup of vegetable shortening until hot. Add a chopped medium onion, and cook for just a couple of minutes, until the onion is soft. Add the potatoes and fry over a medium-high heat, turning frequently, until the potatoes and onions are browned, about 10 minutes.

Then turn the heat to low, cover with a tight lid, and cook until the potatoes are done, 10 to 12 minutes longer. But stay on top of them! I know from experience they can be fine one second and then your nose tells you it's too late—you've got scorched potatoes for breakfast.

WHOLE WHEAT NOT-QUITE-SWEET MUFFINS

◆   Sift together 1 1/2 cups of whole wheat flour, 1/2 cup of unbleached white flour, 2 1/2 teaspoons of baking powder, and 1/2 teaspoon of salt into a large mixing bowl. (For lighter muffins use more unbleached white flour.)

In another bowl, thoroughly mix 1 beaten egg with 1 cup of milk, 1/3 cup of honey, and 1/4 cup of vegetable oil. Add to the dry ingredients, stirring quickly, just until all of the ingredients are moistened; the batter should be lumpy. Stir in 1/2 cup of raisins or walnut pieces.

Grease a muffin tin and fill 8 cups about halfway. Bake in a preheated oven at 425° for 20 minutes, or until browned. Serve immediately with butter and jelly. Makes 8 large muffins.

One cold an' frosty mornin'
Just as de sun did riz,
De possum roared, de raccoon howled,
'Cause he begun to friz.
He drew hisse'f up in a knot
Wid his knees up to his chin,
An' ev'rything had to cl'ar de track,
When he streatched out agin.

—old song used to wake up children

SASSAFRAS TEA

✦   In late winter, when it was nearly spring, Daddy or Grandpa would come back from the woods with their pockets stuffed with bark from the red sassafras tree. If you don't have sassafras trees in your area, you can buy the bark in a well-stocked health food store.

To make the tea, bring to a boil 6 to 8 pieces, two to three inches long, of well-scrubbed bark in a big kettle filled with half a gallon of water. After it boils, reduce the heat to very low and simmer for 20 minutes, or until the water turns red. Sweeten with sugar or honey to taste. Sassafras tea's wonderful orangey rose color and sweet, naturally spicy smell are unforgettable. Makes ½ gallon and keeps for several days in the refrigerator.

In the Spring of the year, when the blood is thick
There's nothing so good as a sassafras stick.
It quickens the liver and strengthens the heart
And to the whole system doth new life impart.

—attributed to James Buchanan Elmore,
a Hoosier poet who was known to
push a plow in his spare time.

Washday Stews

Talk of joy: there may be things better than beef stew and baked potatoes and home-made bread—there may be.

—David Grayson,
Adventures in Contentment

Monday was washday and Mother was in the basement early to get started on the white things. In brutally cold weather it was hard work to pick up each water-soaked towel, sheet, and pair of overalls to put through the wringer of the old Sears and Roebuck washing machine. When my hands got so frozen they wouldn't move, Mother sent me upstairs to check on the stew—our wintertime Monday meal. Even in winter—as long as the sun was shining—baskets of wet clothes were hung out to dry on the three long rows of clothesline behind the house. The cold, stiff arms and legs of our clothes looked like they were being worn by ghosts frozen in midair. Mother always said you could tell the kind of house a woman kept by how carefully she hung out her clothes. Nothing gave her quite as much satisfaction as look-ing at her squeaky clean laundry against the bright blue sky.

Home, and, being washing-day, dined upon cold meat.

—Samuel Pepys,
diary entry for April 4, 1666

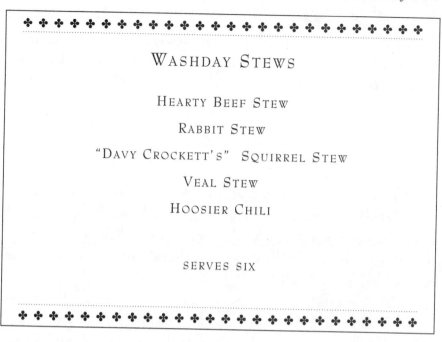

WASHDAY STEWS

HEARTY BEEF STEW

RABBIT STEW

"DAVY CROCKETT'S" SQUIRREL STEW

VEAL STEW

HOOSIER CHILI

SERVES SIX

HEARTY BEEF STEW

✦ Nothing helped us tackle chores in subzero weather like beef stew.

Start with ½ pound of salt pork cut into small pieces. (Use bacon if you can't get salt pork.) Fry it in the bottom of a Dutch oven until cooked but not crisp. Add 2 pounds of beef stew meat or beef tenderloin cut into 2-inch pieces. Quickly brown over a high heat. Reduce the heat to low and add 2 medium white onions cut into ½-inch-thick slices; also add several stalks of celery, chopped; 2 cups of canned tomatoes; 4 garlic cloves, crushed; 2 cups of beef broth or bouillon; salt and pepper; 2 bay leaves; 2 teaspoons of mixed green herbs, such as marjoram, sage, thyme, and rosemary; and 1½ to 2 cups of red cooking wine for a hearty flavor. Cover and simmer for 1½ to 2 hours, or until the meat is tender and the flavors have blended.

Add 3 to 4 quartered medium potatoes and 3 to 4 carrots, quartered lengthwise. In addition, you can add 3 cups of almost any vegetables that you like—cauliflower, green peppers, mushrooms, green beans. I usually throw in whatever I have on hand. (If you use mushrooms, add them after the other vegetables have cooked for 15 minutes.) Cook until the vegetables are done and the meat is tender, about another 30 minutes.

RABBIT STEW

♦   Although there was a rusty old shotgun on our back porch, I never knew Daddy or Grandpa or my brothers to hunt. Still, neighbors would drop off some squirrel, rabbit, or venison when they had more than they could use. Of the three, the delicate flavor of rabbit was the one we liked best.

This dish calls for a 2-to 3-pound ready-to-cook rabbit. Section the rabbit by cutting it into 2 pieces along the backbone and then cutting each half into 3 pieces. Wash and dry the pieces. Salt and pepper and dredge with flour.

In a Dutch oven, heat $^3/_4$ cup of vegetable oil until hot. Brown the rabbit quickly on all sides. Sprinkle on a teaspoon of rosemary. Add enough chicken broth or bouillon to cover the meat. Cover and simmer for $1^1/_2$ hours.

Add a handful of small white whole onions, 3 carrots, and 3 potatoes, quartered. Cook until the vegetables are tender, about 30 minutes. Remove the bones from the meat.

To thicken the stew, stir 2 tablespoons of flour into $^1/_2$ cup of the hot broth in a separate saucepan. Cook the lumps out of the flour before mixing into the stew. Add to the stew and stir well.

Transfer the stew to a casserole or deep baking dish and top with biscuits. (You can use the Buttermilk Stir-Up Biscuits from page 28.) Bake in a preheated 400° oven for about 20 minutes, or until the biscuits are well browned.

"DAVY CROCKETT'S" SQUIRREL STEW

◆   During the Davy Crockett craze in the 1950s, an article appeared in one of the Indianapolis newspapers about the relationship of my great-grandmother, Belle Crockett, and her sister, Lillian, to the colonel. We learned a lot from that article! Our side of the family had been cut off from the Crockett side ever since Grandpa had had a falling out with them over whether or not we should have gotten into World War I. Once the article put us back in touch with Davy, it seemed only right to name our squirrel stew in his honor.

If you aren't a hunter or don't know one, a good butcher can get squirrel and dress it for you. If game makes you squeamish, you can use chicken or rabbit instead of squirrel.

Cut 3 squirrels into frying pieces. Melt $1/2$ cup of vegetable oil in a Dutch oven over a medium-high heat. Add the squirrel pieces and cook until browned on all sides. Don't worry if they stick a little—squirrel doesn't have much fat. Season with salt and pepper. Remove the meat and set aside.

Add a chopped medium onion, 2 chopped green bell peppers, and 3 large cloves of garlic, chopped; add vegetable oil if necessary. Sauté until softened. Put the squirrel back in the Dutch oven and add a cup of water. Cover and simmer for 1 hour.

Add a cup of red cooking wine—Davy was known to like his liquor, although red wine was probably a little tame for him. Also mix in a tablespoon of brown sugar and 3 to 4 whole cloves. Cover and simmer until the squirrel is tender, about another $1\frac{1}{2}$ to 2 hours.

Remove the meat and set aside. In a small dish, mix a tablespoon of flour with some of the stewing liquid. When the flour dissolves, add the mixture to the stew, along with 2 cups of quartered mushrooms. (If you can get wild mushrooms they are more authentic, but cultivated ones are fine.) Cook until thickened and the mushrooms are done, about 15 minutes. Pour over the meat and serve over boiled potatoes.

And so one day as I was goin' a-spoonin'
I met Colonel Davy, and he was goin' a-coonin'.
Says I, "Where's your gun?" "I ain't got none."
"How you goin' kill a coon when you haven't got a gun?"
Says he, "Pompcalf, just follow after Davy,
And he'll soon show you how to grin a coon crazy."
I followed on a piece and thar sot a squirrel,
A-settin' on a log and a-eatin' sheep sorrel. . . .
He grinned six times hard enough to git his dinner!
The critter on the log didn't seem to mind him—
Jest kep' a-settin' thar and wouldn't look behind him.©

—from "The Ballad of Davy Crockett,"
collected by Lomax and Lomax

Congress allows lemonade to the members and has charged it under the head of stationery—I move that whiskey be allowed under the item of fuel.

—Davy Crockett,
addressing Congress

VEAL STEW

✦ In a Dutch oven, brown 2 pounds of cubed veal in just enough vegetable oil to keep it from scorching, about ¼ of a cup. Chop a large white onion and 6 to 7 stalks of celery and add to the meat while it is frying. Sauté until browned (it won't get as dark as beef, of course) and add a bay leaf, pepper, salt, 1 teaspoon of dried mixed green herbs (any combination of thyme, oregano, rosemary, marjoram, sage, or basil), 1 teaspoon of dill weed, and a slice of bacon for flavoring. Add 1 cup of white cooking wine and enough hot water to cover the meat. Simmer for 1 hour, or until the meat begins to get tender.

Add 2 potatoes cut into chunks, and cook until the potatoes are almost tender and the meat is fully tender, about 15 minutes.

Add 2 cups of sliced mushrooms and 3 zucchini, cut into ½-inch slices, and let cook until the vegetables are done, another 10 minutes. This stew is great over Corn Bread (see page 132).

HOOSIER CHILI

✦   Between Thanksgiving and Christmas all of us had different church and school parties: Daddy had his Agriculture Extension and Farm Bureau events; Mother had community shindigs; and we kids had lots of holiday parties. Many of those festivities were chili suppers where men and women alike pitched in to make big vats of the spicy, thick stew, Hoosier style.

Melt 2 tablespoons of butter in a cast-iron skillet and sauté 1 chopped large white onion, and 2 crushed cloves of garlic, until the onion is soft, about 5 minutes. Add 1 pound of lean ground beef and cook over a high heat, breaking up the meat into bite-size chunks, for 7 to 8 minutes. Add a 28-ounce can of tomatoes, a 46-ounce can of tomato juice and a 1-pound can of kidney beans, drained. Season with ¼ teaspoon of sugar, ½ teaspoon of ground cumin, and ground red pepper, chili powder, salt, and pepper to taste. Cover and simmer, stirring from time to time, for about an hour.

Cook and drain a cup of elbow macaroni and add to the chili. Simmer 5 minutes over low heat. Serve hot.

The hoosier has all the attributes peculiar to the backwoodsmen of the West. . . . He was heard to remark that he "didn't see the reason of folks livin' in a heap this way, where they grew no corn and had no bars to kill."

—John Russell Bartlett, *Dictionary of Americanisms*

Christmas on the Farm

Christmas won't be Christmas without any presents.

—Louisa May Alcott.
  Spoken by Jo in the opening words of *Little Women*

Christmas was a magical time on the farm. The silent white landscape of our winters came to life with the sudden bustle of presents, colored lights, Santa Claus cookies, and church parties. The fun really began on the second Saturday of December, when Daddy announced that he had found the tree. Since Thanksgiving he'd been keeping an eye out for a six-foot spruce that looked just right. After we dragged the tree home, we spent the rest of the day stringing popcorn and making pinecone wreaths while Mother carefully unpacked the ornaments. My favorites were a pair of delicate glass swans Uncle Oris brought back from the Far East after World War II and the gold star that my oldest brother, Alan, put on top of the tree.

When the tree was almost finished, Mother came up from the basement with a bushel basket brimming with presents. She had more stashed away than we had even dreamed. Since Halloween she had been hoarding "gifts" to put under the tree. Christmas wasn't Christmas unless one whole corner of the living room was flooded with gifts. Underwear was a sure thing and we always got a full year's supply individually boxed with a perky handmade bow. Everything was fair game to Mother—flashlight batteries, hand lotion, pens, pencils—each wrapped in a different kind of paper. Regardless of how the farm was doing, Santa Claus always left something special under the tree for Alan, Jeff, Sue, and me. We had a rule on Christmas morning: the first one to awaken woke up the rest, so we all saw the gifts from Santa at the same time. After we played for a while with the new toys Santa had left, Mother started handing out her gifts to us—the pretty boxes we'd been shaking behind her back for the last couple of days. With so many gifts to open, Christmas morning went on forever, which was exactly what Mother had planned.

Along about two o'clock we went over to Grandpa and Mamaw Hutchens' for Christmas dinner. Their place was overrun with children and grandchildren looking for the envelopes of Christmas money hidden throughout the house. By five o'clock all of the adults were turning the house upside down and Aunt Paupie was muttering that her envelope had been forgotten, but it never was.

Mamaw's Christmas specialties were a sight to behold: chewy big popcorn balls for the grandkids, roast turkey with old-fashioned sage dressing, her exceptionally plump chicken and light dumplings, potted beef with homemade noodles cooked in its gravy, rich and dark mince-meat pie, mouth-watering hickory nut pie, and a nutmeggy custard pie that she always made ''just for Nancy.'' My birthday was on December 22nd and Mamaw Hutchens knew that sometimes it got lost amidst the other Christmas festivities, so she always made me a special treat. Mother could be counted on to bring persimmon pudding, a dessert that Hoosiers have been having for Christmas since the earliest pioneer days, and the gooiest, sweetest dessert of all: date pudding. My aunts—Pauline, Imojean, and Marie—all came with covered dishes to add to the weight of the table.

After dinner, we exchanged gifts, told stories and jokes, and sang until late into the night. The uncles carried sleeping kids to the cars, while the aunts gathered up their dishes. Another Christmas Day was a memory.

> *Merry, Merry Christmas, everywhere,*
> *Cheerily it ringeth through the air,*
> *Christmas bells, Christmas trees,*
> *Christmas odors on the breeze.*
>
> —Christmas song

✣ ✣

CHRISTMAS ON THE FARM

THE SNACKS

> MAMAW HUTCHENS' POPCORN BALLS
>
> NUT AND GRAIN PARTY MIX
>
> THE EASIEST CHEESE BALL

THE MAIN COURSE

> ROAST TURKEY AND SWEET SAGE DRESSING
>
> TWICE-BAKED SWEET POTATOES
>
> SCALLOPED POTATOES
>
> SWEET-AND-SOUR THREE-BEAN SALAD
>
> MOTHER'S CHRISTMAS CRANBERRY SALAD
>
> MILK-AND-HONEY BREAD

THE DESSERTS

> OLD-FASHIONED MINCEMEAT PIE
>
> HICKORY NUT PIE
>
> NUTMEGGY CUSTARD PIE
>
> PERSIMMON PUDDING
>
> DATE PUDDING

SERVES VARIOUS NUMBERS

✣ ✣

MAMAW HUTCHENS' POPCORN BALLS

+   Make 2½ gallons of salted popcorn.

In a heavy saucepan, mix together ¼ cup of dark molasses, 2 cups of sugar, ½ cup of hot water, 2 tablespoons of white vinegar, and ¼ cup of milk. Cook over a medium heat, stirring constantly, until the mixture boils and registers 250° on a candy thermometer (the hard-ball stage). Remove from the heat.

Add ¼ cup of butter and 1 teaspoon of baking soda and mix well, using a wooden spoon. Pour over the popped corn and toss to coat. When just barely cool enough to handle, butter your hands and shape into balls.

NUT AND GRAIN PARTY MIX

+   Preheat the oven to 275°. In a small saucepan, melt ½ cup of butter. Add 1 teaspoon of onion salt, 1 teaspoon of garlic powder, ½ teaspoon of celery salt, ¼ teaspoon of paprika, and 3 tablespoons of Worcestershire sauce and mix well. Remove from the heat.

In a big bowl, mix together enough Wheat Chex, Rice Chex, and popped popcorn to measure 3 quarts. Add 1 cup of cashew pieces, 2 cups of salted peanuts, and 1 cup of pretzel sticks. Drizzle the butter mixture over the nuts and grains and toss to mix very well.

Spread on cookie sheets. Bake, tossing frequently, until crisp, about an hour. Makes 1 gallon.

THE EASIEST CHEESE BALL

◆   Soften and mix these cheeses: two 8-ounce packages of cream cheese, 4 ounces of crumbled Roquefort, and one 6-ounce jar of cheddar cheese spread. Add 1 tablespoon of Worcestershire sauce, 1 teaspoon of garlic powder, and 1 teaspoon of onion juice and mix well. Divide the mixture in half and form into 2 balls. Roll each ball in finely chopped pecans. Chill before serving.

ROAST TURKEY AND SWEET SAGE DRESSING

◆   Wash an 18-to-20-pound turkey inside and out and pat dry. Baste the skin with melted butter; rub 2 tablespoons of salt and 1 tablespoon of coarse-ground pepper (or to taste) into the skin.

To make enough dressing (stuffing to people outside of the Midwest) for an 18-to-20-pound turkey, break 1 1/2 pounds of slightly stale white bread into small pieces and soak it in 1 quart of milk until soggy. (Homemade bread is exceptionally good in dressing.) Mix in an 8-ounce can of whole oysters, including the juice.

Chop a medium-size white onion and 7 to 8 stalks of celery. Melt 1 cup of butter in a large skillet over a medium-high heat. Sauté the onion and celery until soft. Add 3/4 cup of raisins and cook for 1 minute, or until they puff up in the skillet. Pour into the bread mixture immediately or they will burn. Add 1 1/2 teaspoons of rubbed sage and a tablespoon of soy sauce. If the dressing is too dry, add more milk; if it is too wet, add bread crumbs. (Sometimes we add a tablespoon of molasses for a slightly sweeter dressing.) Mix well.

Stuff the turkey. (If you have dressing left over, you can bake it in a greased baking dish at 350° for 30 to 45 minutes—depending on the amount—until it is browned on top.) Fold the wings under the back and place the turkey on a rack in a roasting pan. Roast the turkey, uncovered, at 400° for 15 minutes.

Reduce the heat to 325° and roast for about 6 hours, or until it reaches an internal temperature of 185° on a meat thermometer stuck deep inside the thigh. Baste the turkey with its own juices every half-hour. When the top is golden brown, cover it with an aluminum foil tent to prevent further browning. A 20-pound turkey will give you 35 to 40 servings—enough for seconds.

TWICE-BAKED SWEET POTATOES

✦   Scrub 12 sweet potatoes. Bake in a preheated 375° oven until tender, about an hour. Leave the oven on.

Cut each sweet potato down the center and spoon out the meat, keeping the potato shells intact. Mash the cooked sweet potato with $\frac{1}{2}$ cup of butter, 2 teaspoons of salt, and a teaspoon of cinnamon until it is the consistency of mashed potatoes. Whip 1 cup of heavy cream. Fold it into the mashed potatoes and spoon the mixture back into the sweet potato shells.

Bake until thoroughly heated, about 15 minutes. Makes 24 servings.

SCALLOPED POTATOES

✦   Peel about 20 russet potatoes and cut into thin slices. Butter the bottoms of two 3-quart casseroles and arrange a layer of potatoes over the bottom of each. Melt 1 cup of butter. Using a pastry brush, dab melted butter on the potatoes. Salt and pepper lightly. Sift a small amount of flour—about 2 to 3 teaspoons—over the layer. Add another layer of potatoes, butter, salt, pepper, and flour in the same way. Continue until all the potatoes are used.

Heat 2 quarts of half-and-half until hot but not boiling. Pour over the potatoes, not quite reaching the top layer. Sprinkle paprika on the top. Cover each casserole with foil. Bake in a preheated moderate oven (350°) for an hour.

Take off the foil and turn the oven up to 425°. Bake until the top is nicely browned, about 15 minutes. Makes 20 servings.

SWEET-AND-SOUR THREE-BEAN SALAD

✦   In a big bowl, mix 4 cups of barely cooked green beans, 3 cups of cooked kidney beans, and 3 cups of barely cooked wax beans. Add 1 cup of chopped green bell pepper, 1 cup of chopped red bell pepper, 1/2 cup of finely chopped onion, and 2 chopped garlic cloves.

Make a salad dressing with 1 1/4 cups of cider vinegar, 1/2 cup of sugar, 3/4 cup of salad oil, 1 tablespoon of Worcestershire sauce, 1 teaspoon of salt, and 1 teaspoon of coarse-ground pepper. Pour dressing over salad and toss. Cover and let it chill for 3 to 4 hours before serving. Serves twenty.

MOTHER'S CHRISTMAS CRANBERRY SALAD

✦   Add 3 cups of sugar to 2 packages of raspberry Jell-O mix. Follow the directions on the package, dissolving the sugar along with the Jell-O.

Using a meat grinder at the medium setting, grind 4 cups of washed cranberries and 4 seeded oranges (with the rind). Just before the Jell-O begins to set, add the ground fruit, 2 cups of black walnut pieces, and 4 stalks of finely chopped celery. Pour into two 13-by-9-inch baking dishes. Chill until set. Serve cold. Makes 24 servings.

MILK-AND-HONEY BREAD

✦   Although this is a quick bread, it has more of the texture and weight of a yeast bread than any I have ever seen.

In a saucepan, combine 2 cups of milk, ½ cup of butter, and 1⅓ cups of unfiltered honey over a low heat. Stir until the honey dissolves, but don't let the milk boil. Remove from the heat. Pour into a mixing bowl and let cool to room temperature. Beat in 4 eggs, one at a time, until well blended.

On a sheet of waxed paper, sift together 3 cups of unbleached white flour, 2 cups of whole wheat flour, 2 tablespoons of baking powder, and 2 teaspoons of salt. Add 1 cup of toasted wheat germ. Using an electric mixer at medium speed, gradually add the dry ingredients to the milk and honey mixture and mix well for about 1½ minutes. Stir in 2 cups of black walnut pieces.

Pour into 2 greased loaf pans. Bake in a preheated 325° oven until the tops are browned, about an hour. Each loaf serves about ten people. The recipe can easily be halved to make 1 loaf.

OLD-FASHIONED MINCEMEAT PIE

✦   Making mincemeat was a laborious but fun project that we would undertake about a month before Christmas. This is Mamaw Hutchens' original recipe, which she always said went "way back." As mincemeat recipes go, this one is relatively simple, but rich and delicious.

Put the following ingredients through a meat grinder, using the medium disk: 2 pounds of round steak cut into 2-inch pieces and boiled until tender (about 30 minutes) and 4 pounds of cored and peeled apples (use a tart apple like Winesap or York).

Mix the ground ingredients with 2 pounds of brown sugar, 2 pounds of golden raisins, 2 pounds of currants, 6 ounces of candied citron, and 1 quart of apple cider. Cook the mixture over low heat until heated thoroughly, about 20 minutes. Let cool to room temperature.

Stir in 1 pint of apple brandy and mix well. Put the mincemeat in a crock and cover tightly. Store in the refrigerator or a cold place where it won't freeze. Marinate it for a week, stirring it several times a day, then store it in mason jars and keep it in the refrigerator for a couple more weeks. We would use the mincemeat for Christmas pies and then freeze what was left over in rigid plastic freezer containers. Makes filling for 7 pies.

To make mincemeat pies, add 1 teaspoon of cinnamon, $1/2$ teaspoon of mace, and a pinch of ground nutmeg and cloves (or to taste), and stir in another $1/4$ cup of apple brandy to 3 cups of filling per pie. Pour the filling into an unbaked piecrust (see page 34), dot with butter, and cover with a top crust. Cut slits in the top. Bake on the lowest rack of a preheated 425° oven until the crust is browned, about 45 minutes.

HICKORY NUT PIE

✦   On Sundays in the fall we would all go into the woods behind the house and look for hickory nuts. Gathering them was easy—they were so plentiful, we always found more than we needed. But then, for the next several weeks, Daddy and my brothers would spend the evenings carefully picking the meat out of the hulls. They were stored in glass jars and used for special meals like Christmas.

Thoroughly mix 1 cup of chopped hickory nuts (walnuts can be substituted if hickory nuts aren't available), 1 cup of light corn syrup, 1 cup of sugar, 3 beaten eggs, 1 teaspoon of vanilla, and a pinch of salt.

Pour into an unbaked piecrust (see page 34). Bake in a preheated moderate oven (375°) until set and brown, about 45 minutes.

NUTMEGGY CUSTARD PIE

✦   This was my favorite pie—smooth and delicate, with just enough nutmeg. Mamaw Hutchens always said she loved me because I was so easy to please. This custard pie takes about a minute to prepare!

Stir 2 eggs together with $\frac{1}{2}$ cup of sugar, a cup of milk, a pinch of salt, and $\frac{1}{4}$ teaspoon of nutmeg. Pour into an unbaked piecrust. Bake in a preheated oven at 350° until the custard is thick and slightly browned on top, about 40 minutes.

PERSIMMON PUDDING

✦   You can use either wild or cultivated persimmons to make this pudding, but cultivated persimmons are easier. Make sure the persimmons are ripe—that means *very* soft.

Scoop out about 2 cups of persimmon pulp from the fruit and pick out any pieces that are too stringy. (If you use wild persimmons, rub them through a colander to eliminate the seeds and strings. You don't need to use a colander with cultivated persimmons.)

Mix 3 eggs with the persimmon pulp and add 2 cups of flour, 2 cups of sugar, 2 teaspoons of baking powder, $\frac{1}{4}$ teaspoon of baking soda, 2 teaspoons of salt, and 2 teaspoons of combined sweet spices—cinnamon, nutmeg, ground cloves, and allspice. Beat in 3 cups of milk, one cup at a time.

Pour the batter into an ungreased 13-by-9-inch baking pan. Bake in a preheated oven at 350° until the pudding is firm and turns a dark reddish-brown color, about an hour. In the first half-hour of baking it will puff up and then collapse into a heavy, dense, very moist texture. Serve with sweetened whipped cream. Makes 12 to 14 servings.

DATE PUDDING

✦   This is a spectacularly rich and incredibly delicious dessert, perfect for Christmas dinners.

Mix together 1 cup of date halves, 1 cup of black walnut pieces, 1 cup of packed brown sugar, 1½ cups of flour, 2 teaspoons of baking powder, ⅔ cup of water, and 2 tablespoons of melted butter.

Spread the dough into a greased 13-by-9 inch baking dish; this dough is very thick, it won't spread easily and probably won't cover the entire bottom of the pan.

Mix together 2 cups of packed brown sugar, 2 tablespoons of butter, and 3 cups of hot water until the butter melts and the sugar dissolves slightly. Pour into the pan over the dough.

Bake the pudding in a preheated 350° oven until brown and crusty, 35 to 40 minutes. The liquid mixes with the dough during baking to become a rich, dark, gooey sauce that saturates a crusty, nut-and-date-filled dough. Another warning: This *must* be served with sweetened whipped cream. One pan makes 12 to 14 servings.

Makin' Fudge 'n Keepin' Busy

*This is the Law of the Yukon, that only the
    Strong shall thrive;
That surely the Weak shall perish, and only the
    Fit survive.*

        —Robert Service,
            "The Law of the Yukon"

Grandpa built the old barn in the thirties to store hay and protect the calves. It was far back in the woods, a mile from our house. When the lane was clear, Daddy and Grandpa bounced along on the tractor, but during blizzards there was no other way to get there except to walk, fighting the driving winds and snow every step of the way. Regardless of the weather, the calves had to be fed and watered.

During the worst snow storms when no one could see a thing and the wind roared right into the house through the window casings, Mother tried to be brave. Although Daddy knew every rock and ridge of the farm, in this weather it wasn't impossible for him to get lost and freeze to death. This had happened to one of Mother's neighbors, Homer Watkins, when she was a little girl in Walnut Valley. She never said anything to Daddy before he left, but we all knew she was terrified. Then she would tell us about poor Homer Watkins, who got lost in the snow and they had to wait until the spring thaw to find him. We made fudge to keep her busy until Daddy got back.

MAKIN' FUDGE 'N KEEPIN' BUSY

PEANUT BUTTER FUDGE

CHOCOLATE FUDGE

BLACK WALNUT FUDGE

PEANUT BUTTER FUDGE

✦   Every time we made candy, Mother reminded us that one of the secrets is to thoroughly dissolve the sugar while it's cooking.

Bring 2 cups of sugar and ¹/₂ cup of half-and-half to a boil over a low heat in a heavy saucepan. Cook, stirring occasionally, until the mixture reaches the soft-ball stage—when it registers 236° on a candy thermometer or when a drop flattens out when removed from cold water. Remove the pan from the heat and place in a pan of cold water until cooled to lukewarm (110°).

Add 3 heaping tablespoons of chunky peanut butter and ¹/₂ teaspoon of vanilla and beat like crazy until creamy. Don't overbeat, though, or it will turn granular. Spread the fudge into a buttered 8-inch square pan and let cool. Cut into sixteen 2-inch squares.

CHOCOLATE FUDGE

✦   Over a low heat, in a saucepan, mix together 1¹/₂ cups of packed brown sugar; 1¹/₂ cups of white sugar; 1 tablespoon of light corn syrup; 3 squares of unsweetened baking chocolate, melted; and 1 cup of half-and-half. Stir frequently until the mixture boils, and then don't stir again. Cook to the soft-ball stage, when it registers 236° on a candy thermometer.

Pour the mixture into a greased metal bowl, add 1 tablespoon of butter, and stir one or two times. Let cool until the bottom of the pan is lukewarm (110°, neither hot nor cold), about 15 minutes.

Add 1 teaspoon of vanilla and beat until the candy is no longer glossy, 5 to 10 minutes. This is very hard to stir, you might want to use an electric mixer. Spread the fudge into a buttered 9-inch square pan, or drop on waxed paper. If it gets too hard to spread, just add a little cream and beat to soften. Cut when firm. Makes about 18 small pieces.

BLACK WALNUT FUDGE

✦ In a saucepan, mix together 3 cups of white sugar, 3 squares of melted unsweetened baking chocolate, a pinch of cream of tartar, 3 tablespoons of butter, and 1¼ cups of half-and-half. Cook over a medium-low heat, stirring frequently, until it reaches the soft-ball stage, 236° on a candy thermometer. Set aside to cool to room temperature.

Add 1 teaspoon of vanilla extract and beat with a wooden spoon until thick, 5 to 10 minutes.

Add ¾ cup of black walnut pieces. Spread in a buttered 9-inch square pan. Cut into squares when firm. Makes about 18 small pieces.

Dear God, be good to me.
The sea is so wide and my boat is so small.

—fisherman's prayer

Soups to Take the Chill off Winter Nights

Winter lies too long in country towns; hangs on until it is stale and shabby, old and sullen.

—Willa Cather,
My Ántonia

*I*n February, when the bleak gray sky and the bone-chilling dampness settled in, we had soup for supper almost every evening. Rich holiday feasts were long forgotten and the garden was not yet in the ground, but Mother's soups warmed us from the inside out. There was her tomato soup, which she made with juicy, home-canned beefsteaks, and her meal-in-a-bowl corn chowder, and her creamy, thick potato soup. Nutritious, inexpensive, and easy to make, these were the foods that kept us going during that long, last stretch of winter.

For months, Mother had been climbing up and down the stairs to the basement to gather potatoes, onions, and mason jars filled with fruits, vegetables, pickles, jellies, and relishes from last summer's garden. But by now, the shelves were getting pretty bare and the potatoes looked as dark and shriveled as walnuts. We had been eating canned green beans four or five times a week since October. All of us were craving fresh food, but we would have to wait another couple of months for the lettuce, strawberries, and new peas. In the meantime we ate these soups, which were Mother's way of lifting our spirits and nurturing our souls. She used to say that, especially in February, everybody needs all the love they can get.

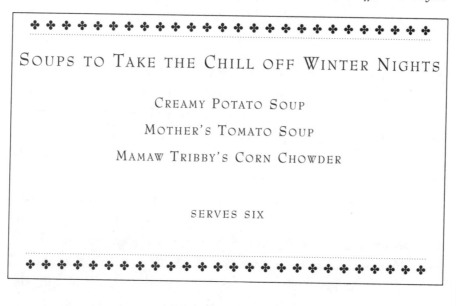

❖ ❖

SOUPS TO TAKE THE CHILL OFF WINTER NIGHTS

CREAMY POTATO SOUP

MOTHER'S TOMATO SOUP

MAMAW TRIBBY'S CORN CHOWDER

SERVES SIX

❖ ❖

CREAMY POTATO SOUP

✦ Peel 5 to 6 medium russet potatoes and cut into chunks. Cook the potatoes in lightly salted water until barely tender, about 20 minutes.

Drain off the water. Pour in enough half-and-half to cover the potatoes, about 3½ cups. Heat it thoroughly, but don't let it boil.

Meanwhile, chop 1 large onion and sauté it in a cast-iron skillet in ¼ cup of butter until translucent, 3 to 5 minutes. Then turn the heat up to high and lightly scorch the onion until the bottom is just barely caramel-colored. When the onion is almost finished, stir 2 heaping tablespoons of flour into the skillet and cook, stirring until the lumps are out. Add ½ cup of half-and-half and stir. Pour the onion-and-flour mixture into the potatoes and stir until thickened. Use your judgment as to how much of the flour mixture to use—you don't want it to be too thick or lumpy.

Simmer the soup over a very low heat, stirring frequently, for 1 hour. If it thickens too much, add more half-and-half. Season with salt and coarse-ground pepper. If desired, you can crumble some crisp-cooked bacon on the top of each serving.

MOTHER'S TOMATO SOUP

✦ I'm almost embarrassed to give you Mother's recipe for tomato soup because it's so easy. The hard part is canning the tomatoes. This soup can be made *only* with home-canned tomatoes and tomato juice because commercial products have a completely different flavor—more acidic and not as sweet—and the texture of the tomatoes is different.

Heat 1 quart of canned tomatoes and 2 pints of canned tomato juice in a large stainless-steel saucepan over a medium heat. Meanwhile, melt 2 tablespoons of butter in a skillet. Stir in 2 heaping tablespoons of flour and cook until the lumps disappear. Add 2 cups of milk and cook, stirring, until heated through. Pour into the tomatoes and cook for 10 minutes. Season with salt and pepper.

MAMAW TRIBBY'S CORN CHOWDER

✦ This corn chowder is best made with home-frozen corn from last summer's garden.

Cut 4 to 5 pieces of bacon into 1/2-inch pieces. Fry in a Dutch oven until some of the fat is rendered. Add a chopped onion to the bacon and sauté until the onions are soft. Add 5 or 6 stalks of chopped celery, three diced russet potatoes, a bay leaf, and enough water to cover the vegetables. Cook until the vegetables are partially done, 15 to 20 minutes.

Stir in a thawed pint of frozen corn and a cup of half-and-half. Simmer until the corn is cooked, about 15 minutes. Mix 2 cups of milk with 2 heaping tablespoons of flour. Add to the soup and stir until incorporated. Add 1/2 teaspoon of sugar to bring out the sweetness of the corn. Cover and simmer over very low heat until the flavors are well blended, 1 hour. Keep an eye on the soup and add more milk if it gets too thick. Season with salt and pepper.

Mother's Sugar Cookies

Those little pigs curled up in a heap,
They shut their eyes and went to sleep,
They slept and slept and slept and slept,
The farmer woke them one by one
And then they rolled out in the sun.

—children's song

*T*he potato soup was getting almost too thick to eat by the time we heard Daddy's step on the back porch. This March evening was special because Tiny, the fattest pig we ever owned, had finally gone into labor.

"Getting that sow to deliver is harder than getting a drinking man to go to church," Daddy said as we sat down to our soup bowls.

As Daddy hunched over his meal, we could all tell how worried he was. Before we knew it, he had snatched a handful of sugar cookies from the cookie jar and was out the door. Just as he was stepping off the porch, Mother grabbed a thermos of coffee and we were off to the pigpen to keep him company.

Out in the frigid night the ground gurgled and oozed, splattering our boots with mud. The pigs lived on the other side of the barn in a hexagon-shaped building with a flat roof. Mother unlatched the gate to the pigpen and we all tiptoed past the sleeping pigs. The pigpen was clean and dry, but I still had to breathe through my scarf until I got used to the pig smell—what Daddy always called "per-r-r-fume." Long shadows snaked on the wall from the one yellow lightbulb that hung over Tiny's huge, shaking body.

As Tiny's labor pains came and went, she groaned and squealed on the hay. Her neighbors weren't too sympathetic and oinked and howled in response. Daddy started yelling, "She's ready, she's ready!" As we watched in amazement, out popped eight little pink piglets, each with its eyes shut tight. Daddy placed them under Tiny's big belly and pried open each mouth to suckle her milk.

Like pieces in a giant jigsaw puzzle, they curled up next to her warm body. After they nursed and Daddy cleaned them, we all held them for a minute and felt the magic of new life. On the way home Daddy carried Jeff in one arm and put his other arm around Sue's shoulders. Mother led Alan and me by the hand. All of us were happy to be a family.

DADDY'S FAVORITE OLD-FASHIONED SUGAR COOKIES

✦   One of the things we could always count on was finding sugar cookies in the big pink cookie jar in Mother's kitchen. Almost every day, Daddy reached into the cookie jar just before heading back to the barnyard after lunch. In December and January, they were shaped like Santas and Christmas trees; in February, hearts; March and April, Easter bunnies; through the summer they were plain big circles; and in the fall—what else?—turkeys.

Cream together 2 cups of sugar and 2 cups of shortening, butter, or margarine until fluffy. Add 2 beaten eggs and mix well. Stir in 1 cup of buttermilk. (If we didn't have buttermilk on hand, Mother would just add 1 teaspoon of vinegar to a cup of sweet milk to make it sour and use that.) Add 2 teaspoons of vanilla extract (or to taste). Sprinkle 1 teaspoon of baking soda and 2 teaspoons of baking powder and stir in. Sift in 7 to 8 cups of unbleached white flour and beat until the dough is stiff enough to handle and cut. Pat the dough into a ball and wrap in waxed paper. Chill the dough for a couple of hours for easier handling.

Divide the dough into fourths. Roll out one piece at a time on a floured board to ¼ inch thick. Cut the dough with cookie cutters.

Arrange the cookies about an inch apart on baking sheets. Place sugar sprinkles on top, if you like. Bake in a moderately hot (400° to 425°) oven until lightly brown on top, 5 to 10 minutes for small cookies and longer for larger ones.

For variety you can add cinnamon and nutmeg or grated lemon or orange rind to the dough, and then sprinkle on cinnamon sugar while the cookies are slightly warm or wait until they are cool and drizzle icing on top. Let the cookies cool completely to let them solidify before you stack them in the cookie jar. Makes about 8 dozen medium cookies.

Leaving the Farm

Go seeker, if you will, throughout the land. . . .
Make it your garden, seeker, or your backyard patch.
Be at ease in it. It's your oyster . . .

—Thomas Wolfe,
  You Can't Go Home Again

From the left, me, Jeff, Mother, Daddy, Philip (Sue's son), Sue,
and Alan's shadow—he was taking the picture.

The morning I was leaving home—really leaving for good—I woke up long before first light and went down to the kitchen. Mother was already up, sitting at the kitchen table in the dark.

"I always knew that of all my kids you had the most wanderlust," she told me. "Don't forget, whatever happens to you, you can make as good a roast for Sunday dinner as anybody. "

Behind her on the kitchen cabinet was a small box with a ribbon on it—my goodbye present. She gave it to me to open while we were still alone. It was a cast-iron trivet that said:

Where ever you wander
Where ever you roam
Be happy and healthy
And glad to come home.

And, although I've lived in more apartments and houses than I can remember, that trivet has always been on the stove, reminding me of the simple happiness and good food we had on the farm.

The City Craze

What! Leave the dear old homestead
　　Where we have lived so many days.
And follow after you children
　　Cause you've got the city craze.
And us so used to country life
　　And common homey cares.
And to go fixin' up like folks
　　Who put on city airs.
Well now, the proposition is more
　　Than I can face.
Why your dad and me would
　　Be entirely out of place.

How could we spunk up and say
　　Good-bye to good old Ball,
Who has turned the sod for us
　　For sixteen years last fall.
Me, leave where I couldn't hear my robin
　　croon in the apple tree.
Nor hear the wren in the rose bush
　　When his song seemed made for me.
The cows are always full
　　You can almost hear them groan.
I think we will stay here
　　And fight it out alone.

To me, a child of nature,
    It'd be an awful jolt.
Like the cagin' of a wild bird
    Or the tamin' of a colt.
My children I give you to the city
    But you in turn give me
The scent of ramblin' roses
    And my favorite pink sweet peas.
I want to hear the cricket chirpin'
    Close beside us on the porch.
And watch the stars a peekin'
    Like a watchman with his torch.
I want to see the baby chicks
    Chasin' and playin' games.
With farmlife's simple pleasures,
    Why who would long for fame?

—Mamaw Tribby (circa 1939)

Index